Dr. Ambedkar's
Vision of India and Jammu & Kashmir

Dr. Ambedkar's Vision of India and Jammu & Kashmir

Aniruddha Rajput

PRABHAT PRAKASHAN
ISO 9001: 2015 Publishers

Published by
PRABHAT PRAKASHAN
4/19 Asaf Ali Road,
New Delhi-110 002 (INDIA)
Tele : +91-11-23289777
e-mail: prabhatbooks@gmail.com

ISBN 978-93-5322-619-0
DR. AMBEDKAR'S VISION OF INDIA AND JAMMU & KASHMIR
by Shri Aniruddha Rajput

Edition
First, 2019

Price
₹ 300.00 (Rupees Three Hundred only)

Printed at
R-Tech Offset Printers, Delhi

Preface

Dr. Ambedkar is known as the architect of modern India through his contribution to India and mostly importantly, his critical role in the making of the Constitution of India. He had a clear and unified vision of India, reflected extensively in the debates that took place during the drafting of the Constitution of India. His imprint is visible on all parts of the Constitution, except Article 370 which relates to Jammu and Kashmir. There are few things said by him directly regarding Jammu and Kashmir, except for his visible absence and silence during the presentation and debate on Article 370. Also, the situation of Jammu and Kashmir was one of the reasons cited in his resignation from the government in September 1951. Except these few references, there is little material that reflects direct statements by Dr. Ambedkar on Jammu and Kashmir. This book aims to understand what was Dr. Ambedkar's vision about India as reflected in his speeches in the Constituent Assembly and other writings and whether and how far that vision has been true in the case of Jammu and Kashmir. In other words, whether his vision of India and expectations have been sidelined in the case of Jammu of Kashmir. I will not give any details in the preface and leave it for the reader to see the book and draw one's own conclusions.

This book is an outcome of interaction and discussions with several individuals and institutions. It is not possible to enumerate them all. But in particular I thank Apporv Shukla,

Yashraj Bundela, Ankit Yadav, Pradeep Kumar, Pankaj Jamtani and Vishal Singh for research support provided on several occasions and very helpful interactions. There have been many others that have directly and indirectly contributed in the completion of this book, I thank them as well. I dedicate this book to those who have contributed one several ways: not just through intellectual interventions but moreover those that made physical scarifies, including the supreme sacrifice of life for ensuring that Jammu and Kashmir remains an integral part of India. Towards the final stages of my books, it was my parents Vasundhara Rajput and Dr. Dhanjay Rajput that insisted that I stay in quiet seclusion at our home in Pune so that the book could be completed in time. They also provided some helpful tips and ideas on the philosophy of writing! They have an important role in the preparation of this book. A book can never be completed without a prompt and efficient participation of the publisher. I am immensely grateful to Prabhat (Goel) of Oceans Publications. They have been patient and diligent, despite several delays on my part.

Contents

1
Introduction

This year the country is celebrating the 125th birth year of Dr. Bhimrao Ramji (Babasaheb) Ambedkar. This is an opportunity to celebrate his personality, achievements and his contributions in making of modern India. Dr. Ambedkar was an eminent scholar and a politician. More than that, he was a statesman and a visionary. For a person of Dr. Ambedkar's stature, appropriate tribute would be to celebrate his thoughts. He made manifold contributions towards realisation of that vision. His views cover multiple fields, prominent amongst which are social, economic, political and constitutional ones. This book relates to his legal and constitutional views and specifically, analyses the constitutional position of Jammu & Kashmir in light of his views on Jammu & Kashmir. This is an occasion to celebrate his vision for India. He wanted to create a unified India with a strong Centre and readiness of the constituents to transcend sectoral identities and sectoral political aspirations. He conceived of India as a strong country with a strong Union that could bring equality, justice and progress for all Indians, irrespective of their place of birth, origin and gender. While we are celebrating his views, we also need to review the present constitutional position of India – whether it sits in tandem with his views of constitutionalism or not. Therefore, this would be an opportune moment to discuss Dr. Ambedkar's view and position of the state of Jammu & Kashmir in the constitutional framework of India. There is a tendency to steer away from issues relating to Jammu & Kashmir on the ground that it is a 'controversial' or a 'political' question. Once a subject is branded such, there is an unwillingness to venture into the subject. Those who tend to dabble tend to take extreme and dogmatic positions. For a student of constitutional law, this subject has to be seen devoid of predisposed notions. Jammu & Kashmir is converted into an enigmatic state with varied claims of special or autonomous position within the Constitution of India. This is an effort to take a fresh look at this issue from the views of Dr. Ambedkar on the vision for India expressed through his notions of constitutionalism. There are many constitutional issues raised in the contemporary debate on Jammu & Kashmir. Dr. Ambedkar had expressed clear views on those issues. The effort here is to look at these views of Dr. Ambedkar and see how far they are realised in the case of Jammu & Kashmir. Therefore, a detailed comparison of the views of Dr. Ambedkar and the constitutional position of Jammu & Kashmir under the Constitution of India needs attention. These discussions impact the constitutional structure of India and address the larger question of integrity of India.

Ambedkar and the Constitution-making Process

Ambedkar was the principal architect of the Indian Constitution. He translated his vision of a strong and unified nation respecting fundamental rights of citizens through institutions and a constitutional structure as contained in the Indian Constitution. His vision for India and the constitutional values that he ingrained in the Indian Constitution were achieved through his participation in the process of the making of the Indian Constitution. Dr. Ambedkar was a member of the Constituent Assembly of India. The democratic structures and constitutional values that we enjoy today are an outcome of the vision of the members of the Constituent Assembly. It was after a century-and-a-half that the people of India would be deciding the future for themselves. They were aware of the challenges the country was facing. The Constituent Assembly was a representative body of Indians that got together to make the Constitution of India. The Congress party had an overwhelming majority in the Constituent Assembly. It was natural since it was the dominant political force at that time. Importantly, the Congress undertook adequate steps to ensure that all sections of the society were justly represented. The Cabinet Mission Plan had given separate representation to Muslims and Sikhs. Other minorities were not given any consideration in the Cabinet Mission Plan. The Congress ensured that representatives of Parsis, Anglo-Indians, Indian Christians, members of Scheduled Casts and Tribes and women were appropriately represented.[1] Efforts were made to induct experts and representatives who did not belong to the Congress – Dr. Ambedkar was eminent amongst them.[2] As the name represents, it is a body that possesses 'constituent power'. Constituent power is the supreme power that is granted by the people of a polity to their representatives to decide their future course. The Constituent Assembly emerged from the people of India and belonged to the people. Therefore, the Preamble of the Constitution, starts by saying, "WE, THE PEOPLE OF INDIA" and in the end, while adopting the Constitution, says "IN OUR CONSTITUENT ASSEMBLY this twenty-sixth day of November, 1949, do HEREBY ADOPT, ENACT AND GIVE TO OURSELVES THIS CONSTITUTION."

The members of the Constituent Assembly are the founding fathers. They deliberated intensely to decide what should be the shape of future India. The Constituent Assembly comprised of people with immense standing and respect. They came from different walks of life. Some were jurists, scholars, legislators with extensive experience, political activists, persons from grassroots and social workers. Most of them had participated in the freedom struggle. They were aware of the problems existing in the country and the challenges it would have to face in the coming times.[3] The greatest challenge before them was to weave together a country that was filled with diversity. The divisive policies of colonial power had left the country socially, economically and politically divided. The centuries of servitude under British had destroyed the domestic economy. People were excluded from real political participation. Society was dived on the lines of caste and the country was suffering from the turbulent and disturbing outbreak of violence that followed the painful Partition. The challenge was to ensure that despite all these problems, the country is kept together and strong. The makers of the Constitution wanted to create an egalitarian society that would accommodate the differences and at the same time ensure that the differences do not conflict with the integrity of the country. There were social goals that had to be achieved. There was a problem of widespread ignorance, lack of education. The long years of servitude under British had deprived them of the patterns of people's participation in governance. India had to be a mature and democratic country. To achieve this goal, some vital social and political measures had to be introduced. The daunting task was to introduce democracy and ensure that the foundational ideas of democracy were ingrained in the people. The Constituent Assembly deliberated upon the political institutions that should be created to realise freedom in its true sense through participative democracy—what should be the scope, powers, responsibilities, nature and functions of the institutions on whose shoulders the burden of democracy was to be laden. The challenge in a Constitution-making process is that the institutions should stand the test of time. Institutions are impersonal and cannot operate by themselves. They are to be operated by people. The attitude and expectations of a society change with every generation. The change of a thinking society entails forethought and a definite course - in which its success would lie—has to be set out in advance. Adequate care had to be taken that institutions do not become hostage to vicissitudes of events, power hungry greedy individuals and sectoral predilections. Most importantly, creation of institutions was not the end in itself for the Constitution-makers. Institutions had to be created for a purpose, especially keeping in mind the peculiar situation of India. Clear thinking on the purposes the institutions had to achieve and how the institutions would achieve them in the best possible fashion was necessary.[4] The Constituent Assembly met these targets. The vibrant democracy of India is a testament to the success of the efforts of the Constitution-makers.[5] The major achievements of the Constitution are in the form of protection of fundamental rights, equality, gender equality, equality in public employment, parliamentary democracy, structures of governance and unity and integrity of the country. Fundamental rights are a watershed achievement of the Constitution. Fundamental rights broke down the walls that would hamper human progress and obstruct the achievement of fuller realisation of human existence. Fundamental rights ensured equality, eradication of untouchability, gave freedom of movement and settlement across India. The end result to be achieved was of all-round progress of all, without discrimination. Granville Austin aptly describes the task the Constitution makers performed in the following words:

> "India's founding fathers and mothers established in the Constitution both the nation's ideals and the institutions and processes for achieving them. The ideals were national unity and integrity and a democratic and equitable society. The new society was to be achieved through a social-economic revolution pursued with a democratic spirit using constitutional, democratic institutions...unity, social revolution, and democracy as the three strands of a seamless web. The founders believed that none of these goals was to be pursued, not could be achieved, separately. They were mutually dependent and had to be sought together."[6]

The Constituent Assembly deliberated for three years before finalising the Constitution of India. It held 11 sessions over this period of 165 days, out of which 114 days were spent on deliberating on the Draft Constitution. The procedure of the Constituent Assembly was that it firstly passed a resolution that set out the vision for the Constitution. Thereafter, various committees were constituted on important subjects, such as fundamental rights, flag, etc. Based on this material, the Draft Constitution was prepared by the Drafting Committee. Dr. Ambedkar was unanimously elected as Chairman of the Drafting Committee on 30 August 1947. The role of the Drafting Committee was crucial. The foundation of the present-day Indian Constitution—accepted and adopted by the Constituent Assembly after intense debate and deliberations—was the Draft Constitution. The task of describing the aspirations of the people and the objectives to be achieved was difficult. At the time of initiation of the work of the Constituent Assembly, whole moving the resolution setting out the aims and objectives of the Constitution, Pandit Nehru said:

"We have a clear field to work upon; we have to prepare the ground and we have been doing that these few days. We have still much to do. ... the high adventure of giving shape, in the printed and written word, to a nation's dream and aspiration.... And I wish this House, if I may say so respectfully, should consider this Resolution not in a spirit of narrow legal wording, but rather to look at the spirit behind that Resolution. Words are magic things often enough, but even the magic of words sometimes cannot convey the magic of the human spirit and of a nation's passion. And so, I cannot say that this Resolution at all conveys the passion that lies in the hearts and the minds of the Indian people today. It seeks very feebly to tell the world of what we have thought or dreamt of so long, and what we now hope to achieve in the near future. It is in that spirit that I venture to place this Resolution before the House and it is in that spirit that I trust the House will receive it and ultimately pass it."[7]

This difficult task of articulating the vision and aspiration of India, in words, was to be done by the Drafting Committee. There was a lot of background work that had to be done to prepare the Draft Constitution. The debates in the Constituent Assembly show the intense scrutiny that the Draft Constitution had to undergo. Even today in courts, not just the words, but interpretation of commas and colons could affect the interpretation of the Constitution. This task had to be done with alacrity, eye for details accompanied with understanding and appreciation of larger ideas that had to be captured in the Draft Constitution. The Draft Constitution that was prepared by the Drafting Committee headed by Dr. Ambedkar was accepted with only minor alterations. The vision that was envisioned by him was carried forward by the Constituent Assembly.

Dr. Ambedkar was a natural choice to become the Chairman of the Drafting Committee. Dr. Ambedkar was a symbol of struggle of the downtrodden. The quest was to see the socially, economically and politically oppressed and deprived classes to join in the process of national building where no one would be discriminated based on his birth and origin. In addition to his championship of the Dalit cause and deep understanding of the problems facing the Indian society, it was his academic strengths and intellectual rigour that made him the perfect choice for the task. Dr. Ambedkar shared the larger vision of India with all other leaders and was equipped to state that vision in words. He had inimitable academic credentials as he had obtained multiple degrees in law, economics and political science. His startling achievements were two doctorates—one from Columbia University in New York and the other from London School of Economics.

He was qualified and a barrister and practiced regularly as a lawyer before various courts. He was aware of the legal intricacies and technicalities—The manner in which a document would be interpreted in future. The Constitution was to touch upon different aspects of life. It was necessary to have someone who could relate theory to practice and grasp the wide variety of issues that would be required to be organised in the Constitution. His scholarship in the field of law, political science and economics was a perfect combination to lead the Drafting Committee. In his research he had done extensive study of the ancient Indian economic model and contemporary problems faced by the Indian economy, especially in relation to monetary policy. His humble origins and background as a Dalit had exposed him to the unfortunate realities of Indian society. Having suffered at the hands of prevalent vices in the Indian community, he knew where the solutions lay and what institutions were necessary to tackle these problems.

Dr. Ambedkar had extensive legislative experience. The Chairman of the Drafting Committee had to not only prepare a Draft Constitution but also defend it before the Constituent Assembly. Knowledge of legislative procedures along with the ability to give direction to a debate and control it were invaluable skills. He had mastered these qualities through his extensive stint as a legislator and member of the executive. He was a member of different legislative bodies, such as the Bombay Legislature and was on Defence Advisory Committee and Minister of Labour in the Viceroy's Executive Council from 1942-46.

He was one of the most influential members of the Constituent Assembly. He was a part of two more committees in addition to the Drafting Committee, which he chaired. He was one of the 20 most active members of the Constituent Assembly that shaped the Constitution of India.[8] His advice was frequently sought on legal and drafting matters[9] and was a 'learned' member[10] of the Constituent Assembly. He had taken various positions that were not necessarily acceptable to the Congress. He had difference of opinion with Gandhiji over the problems of the backward caste people. Yet, Dr. Ambedkar was invited personally by Pandit Nehru to become a member of the first cabinet.[11] It is only a tribute to his intellect and stature. He showed magnanimity in accepting the offer because he never believed in opposing just for the sake of opposition. He accepted the request of Pandit Nehru because it was unconditional and he saw it as an important opportunity to shape the future of India and most importantly, secure the interests of the backward. They had been excluded from the mainstream and from participation in the main process.[12]

The Constitution was approached from a practical standpoint rather than theory because it was meant to create institutions and achieve social transformation of the country. The Constitution was to be prepared with public participation. The Draft Constitution was open for comments of the public for eight months before it was taken up by the Constituent Assembly for discussion. Innumerable suggestions covering different areas were expected. Additionally, the Constituent Assembly was composed of eminent scholars and jurists. They too had to be satisfied about appropriateness of each provision in the Constitution. All these objectives were to be achieved with the strength of reason and art of persuasion. To undertake these functions, wide-ranging knowledge was required. Dr. Ambedkar possessed these qualities. Moreover, he had excellent grasp of constitutional issues and was an expert of comparative constitutional law. He had studied and reflected deeply on constitutions of different countries. He had closely studied the constitution-making process of different countries. His expertise in comparative constitutional law is reflected in the debates at the Constituent Assembly. There are innumerable instances where, with ease, he took the Constituent Assembly through the Constitution-making process and the political structures in different countries and the reasons why they were so structured. The debates in the Constituent Assembly are replete with the depth of his intellect and the width of his knowledge of constitutionalism prevalent in different parts of the world. He very ably described the nature of federalism in different countries. He explained their drawbacks and rigidities. His command over constitutions of different countries can be witnessed in his speeches in the Constituent Assembly.[13] One criticism of the Indian Constitution is that it is heavily borrowed. Dr. Ambedkar did not bodily lift from different Constitutions. He was careful while introducing concepts from other constitutions of the world into the Indian Constitution. The debates, as discussed in the following chapters, show his effort to adapt the experience of other countries and improve upon the experience of functioning of constitutions in other countries.

The position of Dr. Ambedkar as the Chairman of Drafting Committee made him the central figure in the Constituent Assembly. He has influenced the Indian Constitution in more than one ways. He was an active participant in all the debates. Even before he became a member of the Drafting Committee, he delivered a detailed speech on the Resolution on Aims and Objectives moved by Pandit Nehru. This resolution was to form the basis of formation of the future Constitution. He had expressed views setting out the direction in which the Constituent Assembly should proceed. Once he became the Chairman of the Drafting Committee, his influence was manifest. His direct influence is evident in the discussion that took place in the Constitution. It is reflected in the debates of the Constituent Assembly. He had to defend the provisions of the Draft Constitution. He elaborated the reasoning behind the introduction of particular provisions in the Draft Constitution during debates in the Constituent Assembly and his contribution came out elaborately during the debates in the Constituent Assembly.

In the first reading of the Draft Constitution, i.e. the first round of debate, other members of the Constituent Assembly proposed amendments. The amendments that were accepted by the House were incorporated in the Draft Constitution and then presented in the second reading where the provisions were finalised. The draft that was presented on which discussions took place was prepared under the leadership of Dr. Ambedkar. On many important amendments he expressed his views at the end, whether accepting or rejecting the amendments which essentially got incorporated in the Constitution. His contribution during the discussions in the Constituent Assembly are vividly seen during the discussions on the Resolution on Aims and Objectives of the Constitution, introduction to the Draft Constitution, interventions during debate on the Draft Constitution and responses to the debate on Draft Constitution. Therefore, most of the important provisions of the Indian Constitution bear his mark.

State of Jammu & Kashmir

By 15 August 1947, when India became independent, majority of the princely states had signed the instrument of accession and integrated with India. Lord Mountbatten, the Viceroy, had advised the rulers of princely states to sign the instrument of accession preferably before 15 August 1947. But this was not the cut-off date. Some princely states, such as Mayurbhanj, Kolhapur, Baroda, Tehri-Gadhwal, Bhopal, etc. had not signed the instrument of accession by the time of Independence and they integrated into India after some time.[14] One princely state amongst these was the state of Jammu & Kashmir. The ruler of Jammu & Kashmir, Maharaja Hari Singh had expressed the desire to join India in September 1947.[15] However, Pandit Nehru declined to accept the offer for integration unless Maharaja Hari Singh appointed a democratically elected government under the leadership of Sheikh Abdullah. Maharaja Hari Singh was unwilling to accede to this request. In early October 1947, members of Pakistani Army disguised as tribes entered the state of Jammu & Kashmir. They started marching towards Srinagar with the intention of taking over the state with military force.[16] On their way, they were looting, pillaging, raping women and slaughtering men. When they reached very close and Maharaja Hari Singh was unable to stop their advance, he approached the Indian Government again. He had already requested for military support from India before 21st October, 1947 but his requests were ignored at that time. When he sent a fresh request in view of the imminent threat, Pandit Nehru agreed to help provided Maharaja Hari Singh handed over state administration to Sheikh Abdullah in the capacity of a popular leader, in addition to signing the Instrument of Accession. Maharaja Hari Singh had no alternative but to relent. Instrument of Accession was signed on 26 October 1947 and was accepted by the Governor General for India on 27 October 1947. After this, the state of Jammu & Kashmir became an integral part of India. Soon Sheikh Abdullah was appointed the state's Prime Minister. Indian forces were sent immediately to defend the territories that fell within the state of Jammu & Kashmir.

While the Indian forces were fighting to drive out the enemy forces from Jammu & Kashmir, Pandit Nehru was persuaded by Lord Mountbatten to take the issue to the United Nations.[17] Accordingly, India made a complaint to the United Nations about aggression of Pakistan on 1 January 1948. Intense back-room politics took place in the United Nations. The British, with the help of Americans, were able to turn tables on India. The reality was India was suffering an external aggression but British and American diplomats succeeded in painting a picture that the regions under control of Pakistan had stood up in revolt against Maharaja Hari Singh and Pakistan was simply helping them.[18] Initially Pakistan had denied any involvement but once proof of its involvement was established, Pakistan accepted that their army was involved and took the stand that they were only helping the rebels.[19] There were two vital resolutions passed by the Security Council. On 21 April 1948, the Security Council passed a resolution directing Pakistan to withdraw its forces from the areas and after they have withdrawn India should conduct plebiscite.[20] On 13 August 1948, the United Nations Security Council passed a resolution directing India and Pakistan to observe a ceasefire and maintain peace in the region.[21]

In the case of other princely states, for integrating the princely state into India, after the ruler signed the Instrument of Accession, a body comprising people's representatives would endorse the Instrument of Accession. Legally signing of the instrument of accession was sufficient under the Government of India Act, 1935, but the people's involvement was necessary. Therefore, Congress suggested that people endorse the Instrument of Accession through existing legislative bodies in princely states.[22] Where representative bodies did not exist, elections were conducted to constitute them. This was not possible in Jammu & Kashmir. One third of the territory was in the hands of Pakistan, an aggressor, and the issue was pending in the United Nations. It was not possible to take measures similar to those taken in other princely states. In the meanwhile, the constitutional relationship between the Union of India and the former princely states was progressing very fast and the Constitution was in advanced stages. Considering the peculiarity of Jammu & Kashmir, a temporary arrangement had to be made until the state came at par with the constitutional progress in other states. As a purely interim arrangement – till a body chosen after adult suffrage was not created – Article 370 was introduced to regulate the legal relationship between the Union and the state for this interim period.

Eventually elections took place in Jammu & Kashmir and a Constituent Assembly was constituted in the state. The Constituent Assembly of Jammu & Kashmir endorsed the integration of Jammu & Kashmir in India as final through a resolution passed on 6 February 1954.[23] Section 3 of the Constitution of Jammu & Kashmir states that:

Relationship of the State with the Union of India

The State of Jammu & Kashmir is and shall be an integral part of the Union of India.

Section 147 of the Constitution of Jammu & Kashmir disallows amendment to Article 3 in the following words:

"147. Amendment of the Constitution: An amendment of this Constitution may be initiated only by the introduction of a Bill for the purpose in the Legislative Assembly and when the Bill is passed in each House by a majority of not less than two-thirds of the total membership of that House, it shall be presented to the Sadar-i-Riyasat for his assent and, upon such assent being given, to the Bill, the Constitution shall stand amended in accordance with the terms of the Bill:

Provided that a Bill providing for the abolition of the Legislative Council may be introduced in the Legislative Assembly and passed by it by a majority of the total membership of Assembly and by a majority of not less them two-thirds of the members of the Assembly present during voting:

Provided further that no Bill or amendment seeking to make any change in-

(a) this section; or

(b) the provisions of Sections 3 and 5 ; or

(c) the provisions of the Constitution of India as applicable, in relation to the state, shall be introduced or moved in either House of the Legislature."

Therefore the integration of Jammu & Kashmir into India is complete and irreversible. Furthermore, after the signing of the Shimla Agreement[24] between India and Pakistan on 2 July 1972 no issue remains in the United Nations.

There are various controversies that have arisen and continued in relation to Jammu & Kashmir. These controversies go to the root of the constitutional relationship of Union and the state. Although Article 370 was meant to be a temporary provision but it has continued for almost seven decades. Based on this, some argue that Article 370 ought to be treated as a permanent provision. They argue that Jammu & Kashmir has a special position in the Indian federation because the Instrument of Accession was limited only to three subjects: defence, communications and foreign affairs. On other subjects, the Center of Union cannot make laws without the prior permission of state of Jammu & Kashmir. This gives autonomy to the State of Jammu & Kashmir.

In view of Dr. Ambedkar's contribution in making the

constitution, it would be timely to look at Dr. Amedkar's constitutional vision for India and the state of Jammu & Kashmir. In legal discourse, Jammu & Kashmir is conscribed only to Article 370 and it is assumed that the state possesses a special or autonomous status. The constitutional story of Jammu & Kashmir is much larger than Article 370 and often goes beyond the mandate, albeit temporary of Article 370. The subject needs to be assessed holistically and in the light of views of Dr. Ambedkar.

Ambedkar and Jammu & Kashmir

The challenge at the time of Independence was to integrate the princely states into India to make a unified country, otherwise the country would have looked like a patchwork of territories without coordination or connection between them. The difficult task of integrating princely states was entrusted to Sardar Vallabhbhai Patel as the Minister for the Department of States. V.P. Menon assisted him in this task in the capacity of the Secretary to the Department of States. In a short span of time, they succeeded in persuading the rulers of princely states that it was in their interest that they join India. The process of integration for the princely states was not seamless but ultimately successful.[25] They all managed to get over the crises that inevitably arose in the integration process. The state of Jammu & Kashmir was one such princely state. The steps taken for integration of Jammu & Kashmir, i.e. signing of Instrument of Accession, were same as they were adopted in other princely states for integrating them into India. None of the other states resulted into controversy but Jammu & Kashmir did and it still remains. Dr. Ambedkar was not involved with the process of integration. However, he had definite views about them. These views were inspired with the feeling of keeping the nation together and a vision of a unified constitutional framework where all citizens, irrespective of the part of India to which they belonged, are treated equally.

Dr. Ambedkar was not associated with the integration process of Jammu & Kashmir but had very clear views regarding the state. He was responsible for drafting the entire Constitution except Article 370. The reasons for his reticence in not participating in the debate on Article 370 in the Constituent Assembly is discussed in Chapter 4. The idea behind the book is not limited to discussing his statements in relation to Jammu & Kashmir. The broader objective of the book is to discuss the constitutional values that Dr. Ambedkar incorporated in the Indian Constitution and see how far they are being followed in the state of Jammu & Kashmir. The principles enshrined in the Constitution continue to operate with full vigour and force in all the states of India today, including those that used to be princely states in past. The situation is not the same in Jammu & Kashmir. What are those situations and circumstances, is the subject of this book. In simple words, this book addresses the question: whether the vision of Dr. Ambedkar for India is satisfied in the state of Jammu & Kashmir?

While we are celebrating the vision of Dr. Ambedkar, it would be befitting to discuss the situation in Jammu & Kashmir. The rest of the country has faithfully walked on the path chartered by Dr. Ambedkar. But, have his expectations been realised in the state of Jammu & Kashmir?

References

1. Granville Austin, *The Indian Constitution: Cornerstone of a Nation*, Oxford University Press (1999), pp. 10-5
2. Ibid, pp. 17-8
3. *See* Shibanikinkar Chaube, *Constituent Assembly of India: Springboard of Revolution*, (2nd ed. Manohar, 2000)
4. The example of this deep thought are the Directive Principles of State Policy contained in Part IV of the Constitution. These principles are advice given by the Constitution-makers to the future generation.
5. Granville Austin, *Working a Democratic Constitution: A History of the Indian Experience* (Oxford University Press, 1999)

6. Above note 1, p. 11
7. *Constituent Assembly Debates Official Report* (CAD) Reprint by Lok Sabha Secretariat, New Delhi (2009), Book 1, Volume 1, pp. 59-60
8. Above note 1, pp. 22-4
9. Ibid, p. 28
10. Ibid, pp. 25-6
11. Ibid, p. 24
12. Ibid
13. *CAD*, Book 2, p. 35
14. For example the Khasi Hills State signed the Instrument of Accession as late as 17 August 1948. See Government of India, Ministry of States, *White Paper on Indian States* (Government of India Press, 1950), p. 215
15. Prem Shankar Jha, *Kashmir 1947: The Origins of A Dispute* (Oxford University Press, 2003), pp. 39,47
16. I am not discussing the reasons why Pakistan indulged in this attack since this is not the main topic. An interested reader may see ibid, p.117
17. See the letter from Lord Mountbatten to Pandit Nehru on 25 December 1947, The National Archives (formerly the Public Record Office), Kew, London: DO 142/543
18. Krishna Menon's Speech at the United Nations Security Council on 23rd January 1957, Part 3; Above note 15, 181-84
19. See K. Menon's Speech, Part 1, para 91,128,136 and para 11 of Part 2.; Kashmir: M.C. Chagla's speeches in the Security Council, Publications Division, Ministry of I & B, Govt. of India (1964), p 12
20. *Legal Documents on Jammu & Kashmir*, Jammu & Kashmir Study Centre, 2nd edition, Delhi (2015), pp. 209-215
21. Ibid, pp. 216-19
22. Pt. Nehru's speech 5.02.1948
23. *CAD*, Jammu & Kashmir, vol. 1, pp. 769-93
24. Above note 20, pp. 245-48
25. For a detailed account of the integration of states see V. P Menon, *Integration of the Indian States*, Orient Blackswan (2016)

2
Ambedkar and Challenges of Princely States

Some of the challenges that operated in the background of the Constitution-making activity were discussed in the last chapter. Amidst all these, the most pressing and difficult was that of princely states. This was a challenge with potential to cleavage the country deeply, if not cemented properly and within time. Discussions in the Constituent Assembly and Dr. Ambedkar's efforts for country's unity through the provisions reflected in the language of the Constitution were driven with the objective of addressing this pivotal challenge. The challenge was to introduce a uniform system in princely states (also called states) and other parts of India and ensuring that citizens of India are treated equally, irrespective of the territory to which they belonged, with equal rights of political participation. It is necessary to understand the challenges of princely states and the manner in which Dr. Ambedkar set out to resolve them with the complete cooperation and concurrence of the Constituent Assembly.

Challenges of Princely States

The process of Independence of India was complex and had to be completed in a short span of time. In addition to the complications posed by the imminent Partition of India, the issue was of unifying the administrative structure in the country. The country was divided into two segments: Provinces and princely states. Provinces were under complete and direct control of the British, whereas hereditary princes and rulers governed the princely states. Princely states were a patchwork of around 562 large and small territories spread across India. The princely states covered 45 per cent of the total territory of India and 28 per cent of the total population residing in these areas.[1] Jammu & Kashmir was one such princely state. The attitude of British towards progress of administrative structures in princely states was sombner. This was reflected in the weak, undemocratic and mostly despotic system in princely states. The princely states continued to be ruled by a monarchical system with a hereditary ruler as the head. People were rarely involved in the administration of princely states and in many states even rudimentary administrative machinery was unavailable.[2] There was a drastic gap in democratic set-ups between provinces and states. The decay in the princely states was the doing of the British. Some rulers and prices had actively supported the British in quelling the first struggle of Independence of 1857. The British reciprocated by ignoring their follies. For the entire country to grow at an equal pace, it was necessary that these administrative and democratic deficiencies of princely states be cured. The entire country had to be seen as one entity going in a single direction and apace.

The distinction between provinces and states was primarily artificial, created due to distinct administrative structures in these two areas. The differences mostly related to extent of political participation allowed to people from these areas. But geographically and culturally, India was one entity. Legally and administratively, India was one unit. In situations of war, peace and conduct of international relations the country was represented as one block. There was regular communication and people freely travelled through all these areas. The economic activity in the region was deeply linked. Most importantly, the residents of Provinces as well as Princely States were actively involved in the movement against the

British. The argument that the rulers of princely states had the freedom to decide whether to join India or Pakistan or stay independent ignores the historical fact of the struggle of the people against the British as one entity. The legal fallacy behind this argument has been discussed in detail below.

The vital difference was the extent of control that the British exercised over internal administration of provinces and states. The provinces were run directly by the British; in the case of princely states, the rulers had a great deal of discretion regarding internal administration. The rulers of princely states retained the power to administer internal affairs of their territories but the overall control vested with the British. The overarching control of the British over the princely states was called paramountcy. Paramountcy was a legal doctrine created by British ingenuity to interfere with the administration of princely states whenever necessary. This doctrine ensured that the overlordship of the British continued over princely states as well, although technically the rulers had the freedom of internal administration. The right of British as a paramount power was secured through various treaties and covenants that were entered into between the British and the rulers of the princely states. This power included control of the British over external as well as internal administration of the princely states. Paramountcy gave extensive powers to interfere in the internal administration of princely states.[3]

Lapse of Paramountcy and Integration of States

The legal procedure devised for granting Independence to India was of lapsing of paramountcy, followed by the integration of states into India by signing the Instrument of Accession. The legal procedure was enshrined in the India Independence Act, 1947 and the Government of India Act, 1935. The Dominion of India and Dominion of Pakistan was created by Section 1 of the India Independence Act, 1947.[4] The dominion status was a transition phase until the Constitution came into being and India became a republic. India became a republic with the coming into force of the Indian Constitution on 26 January 1950. In the ordinary course, a dominion continues to remain under the control of the Imperial power. It enjoys discretion in administration, subject to the control of the Imperial power. However, India was to immediately become independent and free from all control of the British Crown. The partitioned territory became Pakistan.

At the time of granting Independence, it was natural to expect that the British would transfer paramountcy to the newly formed Dominion of India.[5] This was in parity with the transfer of power regarding the provinces. Independence entailed transfer of complete power over the provinces; likewise paramountcy should also have been transferred. The British declined to transfer paramountcy to India. This was announced under the scheme for the transfer of power – the Cabinet Mission Plan. The Cabinet Mission Memorandum of 12 May 1946 was to become the basis for transfer of power. It declined transfer of paramountcy in the following words:

"2. During the interim period, which must elapse before the coming into operation of a new constitutional structure under which British India will be independent or fully self-governing, paramountcy will remain in operation. But the British Government could not and will not in any circumstances transfer paramountcy to an Indian Government."[6]

It is assumed that the non-transfer of paramountcy by British to Indian Government gave the choice to princes to stay independent. Dr. Ambedkar strongly disagreed with this theory. Objecting to the so-called lapse of paramountcy, he argued that once the Government of India fits into the shoes of the British Government there was no question of paramountcy lapsing. Indian Government will be taking over the position of the old ruler and therefore the substituting government will automatically succeed to paramountcy.[7] The princely states could never become independent in law. They would remain under the control of the newly formed Government of India which would replace the British Crown and then no other country in the world can recognise the princely states as independent.[8] Dr. Ambedkar summarised his position in the following words:

"It would be wise on the part of the Indian states to follow that line and not to pursue the mirage of Independence. The people of India should, therefore, repudiate the proposition enunciated by the Cabinet Mission that paramountcy will lapse."[9]

Dr. Ambedkar explained that claims of Independence due to lapse of paramountcy were untenable. He explained that legally and practically that was not possible. He said:

"To be independent and to hope to get recognition and protection from the UNO is to live in one's own paradise. It is doubtful if the UNO will give recognition to Indian states ignoring the claim by India of suzerainty over them. But even if that happens, the UNO will never grant any assistance to an Indian state from external aggression or internal commotion without insisting that the state should first introduce responsible government within its area. All these things are writ large on the wall. He who runs may read it. Those who refuse to read it will no doubt share the fate which befalls all those who are blinded by their self-interest."[10]

The Congress in its Resolution of 15 July 1947 expressly rejected the effect of lapsing of paramountcy, i.e. the princely states would automatically become independent.[11] The Resolution resonated views of Dr. Ambedkar. This was also the understanding of the British. The Cabinet Mission Plan was explained by Lord Mountbatten to the representative body of rulers, called the Chamber of Princes. In his address to the Chamber of Princes on 25 July 1947, Lord Mountbatten said that the rulers would become independent on 15August 1947 'technically' and 'legally'. He said that:

"Now, the Indian Independence Act releases all the states from all their obligations to the crown. The states will have complete freedom – technically and legally they become independent."[12]

These words were chosen deliberately because the original system was intended to be continued till the rulers signed the Instrument of Accession. The position of the British Crown was taken over by the state department until the princely states signed the Instrument of Accession. Furthermore, Lord Mountbatten had not promised to recognise the princely states. In order to obtain the status of a country in international law, recognition by other states as a country is important. Therefore, the possibility of being independent countries in the international community did not exist.[13] Lord Mountbatten further elaborated this position by saying that:

" While the Political Department exercised functions relating to paramountcy on behalf of the Crown Representatives, the state departments are to take over those subjects gradually which have noting to do with paramountcy but which will be concerned with relations with neighbouring states and also provide the machinery to negotiate in such matters."[14]

The lapsing of paramountcy was to create a void, which had to be filled by some arrangement. The Cabinet Mission Memorandum further stated:

"This means that the rights of the states which flow from their relationship to the Crown will no longer exist and that all the rights surrendered by the States to the paramount power will return to the states. Political arrangements between the states on the one side and the British Crown and British India on the other will thus be brought to an end. The void will have to be filled either by the state entering into a federal relationship with the successor government or governments in British India, or failing this, entering into particular political arrangements with it or them."[15]

This arrangement was the signing of Instrument of Accession.[16] It was natural to expect that the princely states would join the Union of India by signing the Instrument of Accession. Even the Cabinet Mission Memorandum noted that the princely states were keen to join the future Union of India.[17] In view of the euphoria of Independence in the minds of the people, Dr. Ambedkar was optimistic that the princely states would join India to make it a strong and unified nation. He was confident that they would leave their selfish objectives and participate to build a unified country. He had faith that they would express their patriotism by joining the new Dominion of India that was being formed during the discussions in the Constituent Assembly to decide the future of the Constitution for India. He drew an analogy with the unification of the German Empire under the astute leadership of Bismark. Initially the German Empire, unified by Bismark was composed of 25 units, each with a different character. There were 22 monarchical states and three republican city states. Once they all came together to form a single unit, the differences between the units disappeared and they became one entity. He was emphatic about the role of one Constitution in creating this unified country and aspired that under one Constitution, India will also be unified. In the case of Germany, it took much longer to integrate all those units. In the case of India, the challenge was daunting. There were around 562 Indian states. There was much shorter time to integrate them. Ambedkar was delighted that India had achieved that target in a very short time. He appealed to the states to immediately become a part of the Indian Union and join the Constituent Assembly so that they would not be required to draft independent constitutions.[18]

A standard Instrument of Accession was issued. All princely states, including the state of Jammu & Kashmir, signed the Instrument of Accession. Jammu & Kashmir, signed the Instrument of Accession on 26 October 1947. The Governor General, Lord Mountbatten accepted the Instrument of Accession on 27 October 1947, thereby completing the integration process of Jammu & Kashmir into India. The Instrument of Accession was the document that the ruler had to sign to join India. The Instrument of Accession completely integrated the princely state into the Government of India. It also stipulated legislative relationship between the Centre and the State. Defense, foreign affairs, communication and subjects associated with these subjects were transferred to the Centre/

Union under the Instrument of Accession and the authority over the rest of the subjects was left with the future administration of princely states. After the signing of the Instrument of Accession, the princely state became an inseparable part of India.

Equal Treatment of Provinces and States in the Constitution of India

The Constitution was to define constitutional relationship between the Centre and the units. When the Constituent Assembly assembled, the units were divided into provinces and states. The British had continued different systems of relationships between the provinces and states. The task before the Constituent Assembly was to introduce a common system of relationship between Provinces and States. This would have brought about parity between the two. The need to end all differences between the provinces and states was ideological as well as practical. The country was practically one but presence of different princely states had created an artificiality that had to be ended. For introducing uniformity in the country, this reform was indispensible. There was a fear that if the states were left to the devices of the rulers, they might come back or control the administration of the states from background. If the old ways were allowed to continue or routes were left for the old ways to return that would make Independence meaningless for the residents of the states. It was necessary to ensure unity between the states and provinces. The stark difference between provinces and states was the extent of participation allowed to the people. In provinces some democratic reforms were introduced by the British but in the states, the powers were vested with the rulers. The Constituent Assembly was concerned that there should be equal treatment of provinces and states.

The system that was initially envisaged was that there would be a separate Constitution for the Centre, common Constitution for all the provinces and separate constitutions for states. The Constitution for the Centre was drafted by the Constituent Assembly. The common Constitution for all provinces was also drafted by the Constituent Assembly. The constitution for states would be drafted by the Constituent Assembly to be constituted in the states. For larger states, it was viable to form Constituent Assemblies, but there was a challenge of smaller units. The idea was that they would be grouped together for the purpose of forming a viable administrative unit.[19]

In the case of provinces all legislative powers were transferred in favour of the Centre. The constitutional and legislative relationship of the Centre with the states was different. Except Defence, foreign affairs, communication and associated subjects the states retained power over rest of the subjects. This created a disparity between the provinces and the states. An important element of treating states and provinces equally was to have equal status for provinces and states in the Constitution. Thus, all elements of the Union of India would have the same status and would be treated equally.

Dr. Ambedkar was strongly opposed to the initial arrangement. Whereby states and provinces were treated differently and states had the freedom to draft their own Constitution for regulating the internal affairs of administration within the state. According to him, provinces and states shall not be treated differently under the new Constitution. Giving a stern direction to the states, he said in the Constituent Assembly:

"I appeal to those states that remain to fall in line with the Indian provinces to become full units of the Indian Union on the same terms as the Indian provinces. They will thereby give the Indian Union the strength it needs."[20]

Other members of the Constituent Assembly echoed Dr. Ambedkar's concern with the freedom for princely states to draft separate constitutions as well. Kazi Sayed Karimuddin said:

"Sir, I have very serious objections to some parts of

the Constitution. As Dr. Ambedkar himself has agreed, the continuance of the states is not really proper in India, i.e. states or groups of states who will have the authority to legislate or to have separate constituent assemblies. In my opinion, it is really a stigma and a blot on the Constitution of India that even in the twentieth century Rajas, Rajpramukhs and Nizams are allowed to continue and to have their dynasties also continued. All these institutions must be abolished and there should be a similar Constitution for every state. All these states or groups of states should either be merged with the provinces or should be converted into independent provinces."[21]

K. Santhanam stated:

"I agree that we should not have the anomaly of having A class states and B class states which will only cause confusion. If possible, I would like that all these different categories of units should be abolished. There should be only one standard unit Constitution with freedom for these constitutions to adjust themselves to local circumstances."[22]

Ram Sahai also supported this position and said:

"I would like to submit to the House one thing more, and this is that the big states, like Mysore and Travancore, which claim a better position than most of the provinces, should, and I request the rulers and representatives if these states to give up their interest in this aspect, accept the same status as is enjoyed by the other provinces. All the resources, which are not essential for the state, should be handed over to the Centre. One cannot fail to understand that like other states, Gwalior state could have maintained its separate existence. But ruler of that state himself realised this necessity and handed over all his powers to the Centre. Just as the Constitution is meant for the people of the provinces, similarly it should be for the people of the states also. Hence I would like to submit to the House and more specially the Drafting Committee that they should adopt some such device that those Unions, which have assumed the form of provinces ad the big states, which have not merged into any Union, may be able to attain uniformity in this respect."[23]

The Drafting Committee and Dr. Ambedkar were opposed

to differences in regime in the provinces and states and between the Centre and provinces and states because different regimes would govern the relations between the Centre and provinces and Centre and states. This difference in regime, in his view would only be problematic for states.[24] The Draft Constitution was in public domain for debate and deliberations for eight months. During this time, the Draft Constitution was debated in the Constituent Assemblies of the states. It was received with enthusiasm and agreement. Dr. Ambedkar was delighted with this enthusiastic response of the Constituent Assemblies of the States. Based on this response, he expressed the hope that all the Constituent Assemblies in the states would not proceed to draft separate constitutions for themselves and would adopt one unified Constitution for the Union and the states – both prepared by the Constituent Assembly of India. The practice was that the existing assemblies in the princely states were to act as Constituent Assembly. There was an assembly in the state called Praja Sabha, which was democratically elected. In the year 1951, Jammu & Kashmir Constitution was amended by the Regent (Yuvraj Karan Singh) incorporating, among other things, the words, 'Legislative assembly' for 'Praja Sabha'.[25] However, Pandit Nehru declined to accept it to continue and directed the creation of a new Assembly. Since a fresh Assembly had to be convened there was a delay in the state of Jammu & Kashmir and the Assembly could not reciprocate with enthusiasm the Constitution-making process as the other states had done. When the Constituent Assembly was created in the state of Jammu & Kashmir in 1951 it proceeded to draft a Constitution for the state rather than accepting the unified Constitution drafted by the Constituent Assembly for the Union as well as former states. All other princely states adhered to Dr. Ambedkar's request, except for Jammu & Kashmir.

Dr. Ambedkar's insistence on treating the princely states and provinces equally and the Constitution for the entire nation to be created by the Constituent Assembly of India was that the states were archaic in their administrative structures. Democracy was not practiced in these places and the position of the general masses was very bad. Unlike these, the British administered territories, i.e. provinces, had a better infrastructure of education and participative administration and governance. The challenge was to bring the states to the level of provinces. The elementary challenge was to allow people to engage in the administration process. Democracy in the true sense was yet to be taken to the people from states. It was therefore necessary that the distinction between states and provinces was removed. Introducing parity between provinces and states would ensure that there is parity in the legal systems. There was a possibility that if the states were left to their own devise, the rulers would take control of the governance in these regions. India would be democratic in provinces but not so in the States. To avoid the contradiction and eminent chaos, maintaining a single system was necessary.

Congress was also committed to equal treatment of provinces and states. Reminding this, Sardar Patel said in the Constituent Assembly:

"I take the liberty to remind the House that at the Haripura Session, the Congress in 1938, defined its objective in respect of the states as follows:

"The Congress stands for the same political, social and economic freedom in the states as in the rest of India and considers the states as integral parts of India which cannot be separated. The Purna Swaraj or complete Independence, which is the objective of the Congress is for the whole of India, inclusive of the states, for the integrity and unity of India must be maintained in freedom as it has been maintained in subjection. The only kind of federation that can be acceptable to the Congress is one in which the states participate as free units, enjoying the same measure of democratic freedom as the rest of India.'

"I am sure the House will agree with me when I say that the provisions which we are now placing before the House embody in them full achievement of that objective. (Cheers)"[26]

Disparity between provinces and states was reflected in

the freedom to draft internal constitutions. The states as well as the provinces were allowed to have their state Constitution The Union would have an overarching Constitution. Model constitutions for provinces were prepared and the states would constitute Constituent Assemblies and prepare their Constitution. This would have created a federal structure with limited powers with the Union. Dr. Ambedkar was opposed to a weak federation. His views about the Indian federation are discussed in the next chapter. He preferred a strong Centre. The representatives of princely states in the Constituent Assembly of India were supportive of Dr. Ambedkar's idea of a strong Centre. Shrimati Annie Mascarene, representing Travancore & Cochin Union, said:

"There is one point which strikes me as being of great importance and that is the centralisation of power. No nation, no empire had survived in the world without a strong centralisation of power. The confederation of Germany as moulded by Bismark today finds a place so difficult on the map of Europe that European administrators find it a problem to dismember them. The examples of Venezelos in Greece and Sun Yat Sen in China are enough to convince us that this Bismark of India is an administrator whose wisdom and experience are unequalled. The states people are very much obliged to the states ministry for the work they have done during the last few months."[27]

She went further to express the hope that with a strong Centre the differences between provinces and states would come to an end. She said:

"We should congratulate ourselves that this is the first occasion in the history of the world when four hundred millions of people have launched on the ocean of self-government and that is going to be the best example ever known in the history of the world. I thank the states ministry once again and request the people of the states under development to rise equal to the occasion and come soon on a par with the provinces so that by next year, we shall have no states but only provinces in a democratic India."[28]

The provinces had agreed that the Constituent Assembly of India should prepare a single Constitution and they would not proceed to draft constitutions for provinces. Their consent to a common Constitution was automatic. The states on the other hand, constituted Constituent Assemblies to draft their internal constitutions. If the states had persisted, then two different systems would have operated in the country. It was practical that the Constituent Assembly of India drafted one Constitution universally applicable in the country since it had representatives from the former princely states. Dr. Ambedkar said:

"They will save themselves the bother of starting their own Constituent Assemblies and drafting their own separate Constitution and they will lose nothing that is of value to them. I feel hopeful that my appeal will not go in vain and that before the Constitution is passed, we will be able to wipe off the differences between the provinces and the Indian states."[29]

The fear in allowing the states to draft their own Constitution was that the rulers might interfere with the Constitution-making process and ensure that their position remains unaltered. For fostering democracy in states – where it was imminently lacking – this system was not ideal. Other states that had constituted Constituent Assemblies followed Dr. Ambedkar's advice. They agreed that a Constitution be drafted for them, which would be integrated into the Constitution of India. This would save the states from indulging in the exercise of drafting a Constitution, under the fear of interference by the former ruler. Accordingly, Vellodi Committee was constituted to draft a model Constitution for the states. The states adopted this Constitution and the Constitution was incorporated in the Indian Constitution thus completely removing remaining differences between provinces and states.[30]

The states found this procedure appropriate since they had their representatives in the Constituent Assembly of

India. The representatives of states would protect the interest of the people of the states. As the Constitution-making process progressed and the representatives of princely states were present in the Constituent Assembly of India, there was quick progress and disparity between the states and provinces was eliminated.[31] The constitutional relationship between the states and the Union was deliberated between the Constituent Assembly and the Chamber of Princes. Chamber of Princes was a representative body of the rulers. Both parties had constituted a Negotiating Committee to finalise the mechanism for participation of states in the drafting of the Indian Constitution and accordingly the representatives of states participated in the Constituent Assembly of India. The princely states entered the Constituent Assembly in furtherance of the agreement between the Negotiating Committee of the Constituent Assembly and the Negotiating Committee of the princely states. The state of Kashmir was a part of this group. princely states insisted that they should be given certain assurances before they agree to join the Constituent Assembly. But no assurances could be given until discussed and decided within the Constituent Assembly. The Negotiating Committee of the rulers agreed that they would join the Constituent Assembly where they would express all their concerns and thus be a party to the final Constitution of India that would be drafted. An important outcome was the allotment of 93 seats to representatives of states. Jammu & Kashmir State had four representatives in the Constituent Assembly.[32] The Indian Constitution was being drafted with the full knowledge, participation and agreement of all states, including the state of Jammu & Kashmir.

The representatives of the princely states joined the Constituent Assembly on the ground that they would behave as a part of independent India. Clarifying this position, Sir Alladi Krishnaswami Ayyar said:

"Then as to the slate: Here again, the states or the state representatives have a place in this Assembly only if they subscribe to the creed and article of an independent India and if they are committed to the task of framing a Constitution for an independent India. Otherwise, they have no place. They must choose to be constituent parts of an independent India or not. If they come in, it can only be on the footing that they are as much committed to the ideal and purpose of framing a Constitution for an independent India as we in what is now British India."[33]

The princely states were continuously associated with negotiations and were an active party in the formation of independent India. They were a part of the process of transfer of power from the British to India as a constituent of India. In the Memorandum on States' Territories and Paramountcy, presented by the Cabinet Mission to the Chancellor of the Chamber of Princes on the 12th May 1946, it said:

"The Chamber has since confirmed that the Indian states fully share the general desire in the country for the immediate attainment by India of her full stature. His Majesty's Government have now declared that, if the succession government of governments in British India declare independence, no obstacle would be placed in their way. The (sic) of these announcements is that all those concerned with the future of India wish her to attain a position of independence within or without the British Commonwealth."[34]

The participation of princely states was not forced upon them. The engagement of the princely states with the Constituent Assembly of India ensured that they were participants in the process. A formula was adopted based on negotiations. Accordingly states were granted representation. The formula agreed under the Cabinet Mission Plan was that the princely states would be represented in the Constituent Assembly once the Negotiating Committee of the princes agreed to participate in the Constituent Assembly. Pointing this out, K.M. Munshi said:

"This is more or less a formal motion for the simple reason that the Cabinet Mission's statement as well as Lord Pethick-

Lawrence's speech, both contemplate that there should be a committee appointed by this Assembly in order to negotiate with the states for the purpose mentioned in this Resolution. I may refer in this connection, Sir, to the recent remarks of Lord Pethick-Lawrence. Lord Pethick-Lawrence said:

"The manner in which the seats representing the states should be filled in the Constituent Assembly was to be negotiated between the Committee appointed by the Indian states and a committee appointed by the British India side of the Constituent Assembly. The states had appointed the committee and when the committee has been appointed by the British India part of the Assembly, negotiations could begin."[35]

The number of seats allotted to the princely states in the Constituent Assembly and the number of seats allotted *inter se* to princely states was based on the size of population. The objective was to provide adequate representation to the princely states. The formula of representation ensured that they were equal partners in the process. The large princely states had dedicated representatives. The smaller states were clubbed with other states to form a group. These were collectively represented.[36]

Due to the participation of princely states in the drafting of the Indian Constitution, the states came closer to the Centre and it was felt that the earlier formula of granting greater autonomy to states should be done away with. Therefore, there was no need felt for the states to continue having separate Constituent Assemblies in the states to draft their own internal Constitution. It was decided that there would be only one Constitution and there would be no need to draft separate constitutions for the states. Accordingly the Constituent Assemblies of Mysore, Travancore and Cochin and Saurashrta accepted this procedure and accepted the Constitution drafted by the Constituent Assembly of India for the states.[37] Expressing satisfaction with the manner of transformation that took place, Sardar Patel, who was responsible for the affairs of the states stated:

"These important developments enabled us to review the position of the states under the new Constitution and to remove from it all vestiges of anomalies and disparities which found their way into the new Constitution as a legacy from the past."[38]

The Constitution underwent various changes due to these developments. The entries in the legislative List of the States and Provinces were initially different. They were dropped. The legislative and executive authority of the Union in respect of the States was made co-extensive with its similar authority in and over the provinces. The jurisdiction of the Supreme Court was extended to the states to the same extent as in the case of the provinces. The High Courts of the states were constituted and were to function in the same manner as the provincial High Courts. All the citizens of India, whether residing in states or provinces, enjoyed same fundamental rights and the same legal remedies to enforce them.[39]

Elucidating the constitutional relationship between the Centre and states and provinces, Sardar Patel said:

"In the matter of their constitutional relationship with the Centre and in their internal set-up, the states will be on a par with the provinces.

"I am sure the House will note with gratification the important fact that unlike the scheme of 1935, `our new Constitution is not an alliance between democracies and dynasties, but a really union of the Union of the Indian people built on the basic concept of the sovereignty of the people. It removes all barriers between the people of the states, and the people of provinces and achieves for the first time the objective of a strong democratic India built on the true foundation of a co-operative enterprise on the part of the people of the provinces and states alike."[40]

While the other states had agreed to this formula, Jammu & Kashmir could not because of peculiar circumstances. Pakistan had attacked the state and a substantial portion of the territory had gone under the control of the foreign aggressor.

It was not possible to immediately constitute a Constituent Assembly and adopt the same procedure as was done in other states. The then existing constitutional arrangement between the state and the Union was allowed to continue till the state recovered from the problems.[41]

Conclusions

The idea of the Constitution-makers throughout was that the entire country is one entity and the difference between states and provinces was only limited to the type of government. It was incorrect to see India into two pieces. Dr. Ambedkar was therefore opposed to any special or differential treatment being granted to princely states as opposed to provinces. Pattabhiraman Sitaramayya was also vocal about this unified vision of India. Animated by the discussion on the need to keep the provinces and princely state on par, he expressed the following views:

"It was in 1936 that I began to take direct and active interest in the affairs of the states because I felt that they could not be kept apart from the provinces of India for any length of time and as I travelled from state to state and cleared thousands of miles by car, I felt that there was no natural partition between the states and the provinces. They were not separated either by forests or jungles or deserts or rivers or mountain ranges, but they were all of a piece with one another and only a tollbar represented by a rope was the dividing line between the two areas and if you travel through Kathiawar which is now called Saurashtra with its 417 states, you cannot pass any two miles without changing over from state to province and province to state. That was an impossible state of things. How it had come into being was unimaginable and there was no point in postponing the consideration of the amalgamation of the provinces and the states."[42]

The challenge of princely states was successfully addressed by introducing a uniform system of administration and indistinguishable constitutional relationship between the Union of India and all the segments that constituted the Union, whether princely states or otherwise. With regard to all the princely states this vision of Dr. Ambedkar was realised and complete uniformity between all the states was achieved. The only former princely state that did not adhere to vision of Dr. Ambedkar and resulted into multiple anomalies is the state of Jammu & Kashmir. It is only in this state that Dr. Ambedkar's vision for resolving the challenges of princely states and been disregarded.

The demand for equal treatment was from the members of the Constituent Assembly as well as the representatives of princely states. Ram Sahai noted this fact in his speech before the Constituent Assembly as follows:

"Only last year a convention of the representatives of the states in the Constituent Assembly was held in Delhi. The statement issued by that Convention also demanded that provisions should be made in the Constitution at an early date so as to put the states and the provinces on the same level. It was as a result of that, that a committee to draw up a model Constitution was appointed under the States Ministry and it drew up such a model Constitution. But the conditions changed so quickly that we find that we have advanced much beyond the model Constitution and we find that the people of the states are getting the same rights as the people of the provinces and the responsibilities and the opportunities of work for both are the same under the Constitution. Moreover, a part relating to the states is being added to the Constitution as recommended by the committee which had drawn up the model Constitution."[43]

Seconding satisfaction over this fact, A. Thanu Pillai said: "The changes that have come about in the relations between the Indian states and the Government of India and the rapidity of those changes are really marvellous. I shall refer just to one fact. A few months ago it was considered necessary to appoint a committee to draft a model Constitution for the states. That means that even then the idea was that the Indian states would have to frame their own separate constitutions. And we have now reached the stage at which we are able to frame the Constitution for the whole of India, including the states, here, and that is an achievement certainly of which any administrator, any ministry, can be justly proud; and coming from one of the Indian states, and I may say, one of the foremost of the Indian states, I am particularly glad that I have an opportunity of witnessing this change and taking part in framing the Constitution, and making the Constitution for the states, part of the whole Constitution of India.

"This brilliant record of achievement should serve as an inspiration to all of us, including the people of the states. As was mentioned here, the states are in different stages of different degrees of development. I am glad that the provisions relating to the provinces are made applicable to the states. The states that are foremost in the whole country owe that fact to their adopting the methods prevailing in the provinces. I mean the administrative and legislative methods, early enough. If Mysore, Travancore and Cochin are now in the forefront of Indian states, that is largely due to the fact that we adopted early enough the administrative methods and the legislative methods that were obtaining in the provinces. The North Indian states lagged behind because they pursued their old methods, and the result is that today we find they are distinctly backward. Therefore, when we adopt the same system, when we adopt the same kind of provisions for all the states and the provinces, we can naturally hope for rapid progress so far as all these states are concerned. Let us hope that will be the result."[44]

All these expectations of Dr. Ambedkar as well as his colleagues in the Constituent Assembly are defeated in Jammu & Kashmir. Disregarding Dr. Ambedkar's directive, Jammu & Kashmir State proceeded to draft its own internal Constitution. It the members of Constituent Assembly of Jammu & Kashmir had taken a practical stand, they could have adopted the model Constitution of states and that Constitution would have been integrated in the single Constitution at the level of the Union. Existence of separate Constitution in Jammu & Kashmir has resulted into various problems. The Constitution of Jammu & Kashmir is neither higher nor at parity with the Indian Constitution. It is no more than a document of internal administration. The anomalies created due to the Constitution and various other unconstitutional actions undertaken in disregard of Dr. Ambedkar's specific directives is discussed in the chapters that follow.

References

1. Government of India Ministry of States, White Paper on Indian States: The Manager of Publications, Delhi; 1950 pp. 17-8
2. Ibid, pp. 1-3
3. Ibid, pp. 22-3
4. Section 1 (I) The New Dominions: As from the fifteenth day of August, nineteen hundred and forty-seven, two independent Dominions shall be set up in India, to be known respectively as India and Pakistan. (2) The said Dominions are hereafter in this Act referred to as 'the new Dominions', and the said fifteenth day of August is hereafter in this Act referred to as "the appointed day"
5. Dominion of India was a state of transition before complete nationhood was achieved. This mechanism was provided through Section 5, Government of India Act, 1935
6. *Legal Documents on Jammu & Kashmir*, Jammu & Kashmir Study Centre, 2nd edition, Delhi (2015), pp. 25-6
7. Dr. B R Ambedkar, 'Paramountcy and the Claim of the Indian States to be Independent' in *Dr. Babasaheb Ambedkar: Writings and Speeches*, Vol. 2, (Education Department, Government of Maharashtra, 1993), pp. 199-203
8. Ibid, p. 204
9. Ibid
10. Ibid, pp. 204-5
11. Above note 6, p. 28
12. Ibid, p. 30
13. On recognition of states in international law *see* Ian Brownlie,

Principles of Public International Law (7th edn, OUP, 2008), pp. 85-92. Hyderabad tried to seek statehood at the United Nations by filing a complaint with the Security Council. Hyderabad was never granted the status of a country in the United Nations. Eric Lewis Beverley, *Hyderabad, British India and the World: Muslim Networks and Minor Sovereignty, c 1850-1950* (Cambridge University Press, 2015), pp. 54-6

14. Above note 6, p. 31
15. Ibid, p. 27
16. Section 6, Government of India Act, 1935
17. Above note 6, p. 25
18. Constituent Assembly Debates Official Report (*CAD*) Reprint by Lok Sabha Secretariat, New Delhi (2009), Book 2, pp. 42
19. Above note 1, Part V, p. 39
20. *CAD*, Book 1, pp. 32-33
21. Above note 18, p. 242
22. Ibid, p. 265
23. Ibid, p. 269
24. Ibid, p. 42
25. Daya Sagar, *Jammu & Kashmir—A Victim*, Ocean Paperbacks, New Delhi (2015). In the state of Jammu & Kashmir the House comprising a popular representation was called Praja Sabha. The Praja Shaba, a representative institution of the state, continued functioning till 1963. It was dissolved thereafter. Normally, the Praja Sabha was to perform the function of the Constituent Assembly but it was dissolved at the insistence of Sheikh Abdullah, who was keen to pack the Constituent Assembly with his party men.
26. *CAD*, Book 5, 12 October 1949, p. 168
27. Ibid, p. 174
28. Ibid
29. Above note 19, pp. 33
30. Above note 1, pp. 108-11
31. Above note 25, p. 162
32. Report of the committee appointed to negotiate with the States Negotiating Committee, dated 24 April 1947 (Presented on 28 April, 1947) published in Constituent Assembly of India, Reports of Committees (First Series), 1947 (From December, 1946 to July, 1947) (Manager of Publications, Delhi, India: The Manager, Government of India Press, New Delhi, India, 1948), pp. 6-9

33. Above note 19, p. 142
34. Ibid, p. 270
35. Ibid, p. 156
36. Ibid, p. 161
37. Above note 25, pp. 162-3
38. Ibid, p. 162
39. Ibid, pp. 163-4
40. Ibid, p. 164
41. Ibid, p. 163
42. Ibid, pp. 168-9
43. Ibid, p. 171
44. Ibid, p. 172

3

Ambedkar's Concept of India

The challenge before the Constituent Assembly was to weave together a unified country that possessed multiple diversities. The situation at the time of Independence was such that the country was divided on multiple lines, the most challenging being the difference between states and provinces. Dr. Ambedkar's vision ensured that the problem of princely states is solved and they get completely integrated into the new India in a manner that their prior independent existence gets assimilated into a new and unified national identity. Building on the cooperation of the princely states, he created a system with limited federalism, where the Centre was strong. The federal structure that he adopted for India is unique and aimed at ensuring that the country stays together despite diversities. Dr. Ambedkar had a clear and precise vision for India which he translated into action through provisions in the Constitution.

Dr. Ambedkar's vision for India could be understood through three broad themes contained in the Constitution or reflected in the debates in the Constituent Assembly. First, seat of sovereignty. This was an important question. Considering the experience of servitude for centuries under foreign rule and hereditary princes, it was necessary to make it clear that the owners of sovereignty had changed. Sovereignty belonged to the people of India collectively. It did not belong to any specific person or a group of persons or a segment of society. Collective possession of sovereignty by the Indian people was necessary for empowering the masses and also to ensure that regional or sectoral aspirations do not spur by claiming sovereign powers for a region. Second, concept of federation under the Constitution. India adopts federal structure but is different from all other federations in the world. It is characterised by a strong Centre. The way in which Indian federation is crafted by Dr. Ambedkar is the second theme. The third theme is the strong Centre. The reasons for which Dr. Ambedkar created a strong Centre are discussed under this heading. While these three fundamental themes representing his concept of India are discussed, the situation in Jammu & Kashmir in relation to these themes is also discussed at the relevant places.

Ambedkar and *Situs* of Sovereignty

Dr. Ambedkar's concept of India is encapsulated in the seat of sovereignty. Seat of sovereignty means the place where sovereignty of India rests. He declared that under the Constitution, the sovereignty rests with the people of India as a whole. It does not reside with the Government of India. Government of India; only represents and exercises the sovereign power in the name of the people of India. Sovereignty does not rest with any state government. He was strongly opposed to the idea of princely states or the former rulers possessing sovereignty. If princely states were allowed to retain sovereignty then that would defeat the idea of India and the introduction of a true and effective participatory democracy in India. He did not support the idea that the constituent units of India, i.e. the states under the Constitution possess sovereignty.[1] If state governments possessed or exercised sovereignty, it would weaken the Centre and make the Union of India fragile. Dr. Ambedkar wanted a clear Centre with relatively weak federal units. His views on federalism and strong centre are discussed in detail in the rest of this chapter. Dr. Ambedkar therefore made it clear that sovereignty under the Constitution resided with the people of India collectively.

No group of persons or one person can claim sovereignty.

Sovereignty is defined in the famous *Island of Plams Case* by Judge Huber as: "Sovereignty in relation to a portion of the surface of the globe is the legal condition necessary for the inclusion of such portion in the territory of any particular state." He further added:

"Sovereignty in the relations between states signifies independence. Independence in regard to a portion of the globe is the right to exercise therein, to the exclusion of any other state, the functions of a state. The development of the national organisation of states during the last few centuries and, as a corollary, the development of international law, have established this principle of the exclusive competence of the state in regard to its own territory in such a way as to make it the point of departure in settling most questions that concern international relations.....The fact that the functions of a state can be performed by any state within a given zone is on the other hand, precisely the characteristic feature of the legal situation pertaining in those parts of the globe which, like the high seas or lands without a master, cannot or do not yet form the territory of a state."[2]

Sovereignty in other words is the supreme and overarching power of a country. It cannot be shared. If it is transferred, then the country loses its existence as a country in international law because possessing complete sovereignty is an essential attribute for existence of a country.[3] There are two aspects of sovereignty: 'functional sovereignty' and the 'seat of sovereignty'. Functional sovereignty is the exercise of sovereignty. The functional sovereignty rests with the government. The government exercises it on behalf of the people, who collectively possess it. Seat of sovereignty means the actual location of sovereignty: with whom the ownership of sovereignty resides. The distinction between functional and seat of sovereignty does not mean that sovereignty is divisible. Sovereignty resides in the people of India and the Central Government simply exercises it on behalf of the people.

The idea that sovereignty resided collectively with the people of India had always been a part of the Constitution-making process. Prior to the stage of drafting of the Constitution, on 13 December 1936, Pandit Nehru moved a Resolution on Aims and Objectives before the Constituent Assembly. The Resolution on Aims and Objectives expressly mentioned that the sovereignty rested with the people of India.[4]

The Constitution was to be framed by keeping the framework of a unified India in mind. The entry of representatives of princely states into the Constituent Assembly took place after the passing of the Resolution on Aims and Objectives. The representatives of princely states had entered the Constituent Assembly after successful negotiations between representatives of Constituent Assembly and representatives of the rulers. The conditions in the Resolution were a precondition for the entry of representatives of princely states in the Constituent Assembly.

During the debates in the Constituent Assembly, a question arose: Where does sovereignty reside? Shri Mahavir Tyagi insisted that the place of sovereignty should be provided in the Constitution. He requested that it should be said is express words that sovereignty will reside with the people of the country. He requested:

"In the Draft Constitution I find that the residence of sovereignty has not been described. Where sovereignty lies has not been definitely laid down. I want that this may go on record. I shall be content if the hon'ble mover of the Constitution would place before the House either in connection with the Preamble or some other Article of the Constitution, an amendment which will clearly lay down that the sovereignty shall reside in the whole body of the people. The word 'state' has one meaning in one place and another meaning elsewhere. It will therefore not be satisfactory to say that the sovereignty should rest in the states. What does the hon'ble Member suggest? Whether the sovereignty resides in the Union or in the states? From the Draft it is not clear. My amendment therefore seeks to lay down definitely where sovereignty resides or shall reside in future."[5]

Some expressed the fear that if it was not clarified that sovereignty rested with the people as a whole there was the possibility that former rulers would claim sovereignty. Expressing this concern Gopalkrishna Vijayavargiya said:

"I come from an Indian state and I have a particular interest in this amendment, and I wish the House accepts it. There are also Indian states coming in as states in this Constitution. We do not want the Rajpramukhs and others to be there permanently. Of course, as the covenants have been signed, let them be there for some time. But, in the Constitution, we should lay down that even the common people can become heads of the provinces and states, and this will be one of the methods by which we will bring the states into conformity with the provinces. This is an important question."[6]

Other members of Constituent Assembly did not share this fear. They were confident that such a clarification in the text of the Constitution was not necessary because it was implied. The obvious interpretation of important provisions of the Constitution, such as the Preamble would convey the intention that the people of India collectively possess sovereignty. Dr. Ambedkar and the entire Constituent Assembly did not support the amendment because it was implicit that sovereignty resided with the people. Dr. Ambedkar agreed with the observations of Shri Mahavir Tyagi and said: "Beyond doubt it vests with the people."[7] However, the idea that sovereignty rests exclusively with the people of India was not inexorably connected to the Constitution that Dr. Ambedkar did not agree for any additional reference to this effect in the Constitution.

Dr. Ambedkar's views were embedded in democracy where people get complete rights. The ultimate place where democracy rested was people. The government has to be participatory without limitations on the rights of the people. Therefore, for him sovereignty resided with the people. When he referred to people, he had the entire nation in mind rather than a certain group of people. In the case of Jammu &

Kashmir it is being argued that the power did not vest with the people but remained with the ruler, which gives special status and autonomous character to Jammu & Kashmir. It is argued that the Instrument of Accession took place only on three subjects and for the rest of the subjects the sovereignty would rest with the Maharaja and which was thereafter transferred to the state government. Therefore, the state government becomes sovereign.[8] Dr. Ambedkar detested the idea of a ruler or government becoming sovereign. For him sovereignty resided with the people and not the rulers and their successor governments.[9]

The constitutional scheme of transfer of power under the Cabinet Mission Plan was that at the time of declaration of Independence and lapsing of British paramountcy, the sovereignty in the princely states would be transferred to the people of the state.

Once the people residing in the princely states transfer it to the common pool of India, sovereignty would be merged at one place. The sovereignty of constituent units after being transferred to the Union would get merged at the common pool represented by the Centre. Former princely states and residents would not continue to hold any sovereign power once they endorsed the integration of the princely state into India. Sir S. Radhakrishnan aptly elucidated this phenomenon in the following words:

"If the great paramount power which is sovereign in this country by conquest, is now transferring responsibility to the representatives of the people, it goes without saying that those who depend on that paramount power should do what the British have done. They must also transfer the responsibility to the representatives of the people."[10]

The cooperation of princely states in the making of independent India is reflected in the debates of the Constituent Assembly. Sir S. Radhakrishnan acknowledged it in the following words:

"The princes – I count many of them amongst my personal friends – have agreed with the Cabinet Statement and wished to take their share in the future development of this country, and I do hope that they will realise that it is their duty to take notice of the surging hopes of their people and make themselves responsible. If they do so, they will play a notable part in the shaping of our country. We have no ill-will towards the princes. The assertion of republicanism, the assertion of the sovereignty of the people, do not in any manner indicate any antagonism to the princely rule itself. They do not refer to the present facts of past history of the Indian states but they indicate the future aspirations of the people of the states."[11]

Therefore, Congress insisted that in addition to the Instrument of Accession, the people of the state should also endorse the Instrument of Accession. This would gather the power of the people at one centre that is, the union to create a unified country, rather than a group of fragmented segments claiming individual sovereignty. Explaining the effects of the Cabinet Mission Plan, N. Gopalaswami Ayyangar said in the Constituent Assembly:

"Even under existing conditions, the provinces of British India and Indian states have a common Centre which administers such subjects as, under any unitary or federal Constitution for India as a whole, must stand ceded to the Centre. Broadly speaking, sovereign powers over India as a whole now vest in His Majesty, subject to the provisions of the Government of India Act, 1935. Those powers are exercisable both over British India and over Indian states, though the quantum of those powers and the manner of their exercise differ in the two cases. The act of ceding sovereignty, that is transfer of the power which Britain now wields in this country will, therefore, relate to the whole of India. When the Cabinet Mission therefore spoke of cession to the people of India, they must be held to have included the people of Indian states also. (*Hear, hear.*) The Mission's statement, therefore, that when British power is withdrawn, the states become independent, should be construed to mean that such sovereignty as His Majesty in fact exercises over Indian states will stand ceded back to the people of those states."[12]

Sovereignty in the princely states was with the people in those states. Explaining this principle in the Constituent Assembly Biswanath Das said:

"Secondly, their objection is centred round the fact that power derives from the people. They would not admit that power is derived from the people in the Indian states. Sir, paragraph 14 of the Cabinet Mission's statement lays down that after the withdrawal of Britain, paramountcy disappears. In Great Britain, it has been recognised by statutes that power emanates from the people. Parliament derives its power from the people of Britain and the same Parliament is exercising the power of paramountcy. That being the position, I do not see any reason why the state rulers and their representatives should object to these expressions. Sir, after the withdrawal of Britain, there is no reason for anyone to think that India would think of any other form of state than a republic."[13]

Supporting this view about the true seat of sovereignty were the people. Sir Alladi Krishnaswami Ayyar said:

" There is no substance either in the objection raised on behalf of the states in certain quarters outside the House to paragraph 4 of the Resolution that--

"All power and authority of the sovereign independent India, its constituent parts and organs of government are derived from the people."

Is it suggested that in respect of the sovereign independent India, the authority of the provincial parts is derived from the people, and, so far as states are concerned, from the hereditary rules of the states? The Constitution of a sovereign independent India is the concrete expression of the will of the people of India as a whole conceived of as an organic entity, and even in regard to the units themselves, the authority of the rulers can rest ultimately only on the will of the people concerned. The state machinery, be it monarchy or democracy, ultimately derives its sanction from the will of the people concerned. The divine right of kings is not a legal or political creed in any part of the world at the present day. I do not believe that it will be possible for hereditary monarchs to maintain their authority on such a medieval or archaic creed. The Cabinet Mission was quite alive to this and in their statement, reference is made throughout to Indians, meaning thereby Indians both of the Indian states and British India, deciding the future Constitution of India, no distinction being drawn between Indians in what is now British tract and what is now native state territory. I need only refer to paragraphs 1, 3, 16 and 24 of the statement of the Cabinet Mission."[14]

Additionally, prior to this position the situation was that the rulers claimed that sovereignty rests with them entirely. The limited power that the elected representatives in legislatures in the princely states – wherever they existed – exercised were a gift by the ruler. This idea was completely discarded with the creation of the Constituent Assembly of India. The Constituent Assembly consisted of representatives of the people, who are the ultimate repositories of sovereignty. Therefore the Constituent Assembly possessed constituent power. At the time of Independence, the sovereignty got ceded from the British Crown to the people of India. This included the people of princely states. The people in princely states got complete sovereign power. By sanctioning integration of the princely state into the new Union of India, that sovereign power of people of princely states got merged into the national pool of sovereignty, represented collectively by the Union. With this incidence, the independent existence of princely states and existence of seat of sovereignty with the people of princely states got extinguished and merged completely into the republic.[15]

It was the understanding of the entire Constituent Assembly that included the representatives of princely states that sovereignty remained with the people and not the ruler. This would ensure parity between the princely states and provinces.

The understanding that sovereignty rested with the entire nation comprising all persons was engrafted from the time of initiation of the Constitution-making process. Before the drafting process began, in order to give direction to the process, the Resolution on Aims and Objectives was presented by Pandit Nehru, as discussed above. There was some trepidation in the minds of the members of Constituent Assembly. Responding to these concerns, he said:

"I am informed they complain of the following words contained in the Resolution.

'Sovereignty belong to the people and rests with the people.'

This is to say, the final decision should rest with the people of the states. They object to this. It is certainly a surprising objection. It may not be very surprising if those people who have lived in an atmosphere of medievalism do not give up their cherished illusions, but in the modern age how can a man believe for a moment in the divine and despotic rights of a human being? I fail to understand how any Indian, whether he belongs to a state or to any other part of the country, could dare utter such things!"[16]

He convincingly went ahead and argued that the seat of sovereignty was with the people of India. He said:

"Another point has been raised: The idea of the sovereignty of the people, which is enshrined in this Resolution, does not commend itself to certain rulers of Indian states. That is a surprising objection and, if I may say so, if that objection is raised in all seriousness by anybody, be he a ruler or a minister, it is enough to condemn the Indian states system of every ruler or minister that exists in India. It is a scandalous thing for any man to say, however highly placed he may be, that he is here by special divine dispensation to rule over human beings today. That is a thing which is an intolerable presumption on any man's part and it is a thing which this House will never allow and will repudiate if it is put before it. We have heard a lot about this divine right of kings and we had read a lot about of it in past histories and we had thought that we had heard the last of it and that it had been put an end to and buried deep down into the earth ages ago. If any individual in India or elsewhere raises it today, he would be doing so without any relation to the present in India. So, I would suggest to such persons in all seriousness that, if they want to be respected or considered with any measure of friendliness, no such idea should be 'even' hinted at, much less said. On this there is going to be no compromise. (*Hear, hear*).

"But, as I made plain on the previous occasion when I spoke, this Resolution makes it clear that we are not interfering in the internal affairs of the states. I even said that we are not interfering with the system of monarchy in the states, if the people of the states so want it. I gave the example of the Irish republic in the British Commonwealth and it is conceivable to me that within the Indian republic, there might be monarchies if the people so desire. That is entirely for them to determine. This Resolution and, presumably, the Constitution that we make, will not interfere with that matter. Inevitably it will be necessary to bring about uniformity in the freedom of the various parts of India, because it is inconceivable to me that certain parts of India should have democratic freedom and certain others should be denied it. That cannot be. That will give rise to trouble, just as in the wide world today there is trouble because some countries are free and some are not. Much more trouble will there be if there is freedom in parts of India and lack of freedom in other parts of India."[17]

The spirit of unity was commensurately reflected by the representatives of princely states in the Constituent Assembly. They did not treat themselves to be special in comparison to provinces. Expressing this sentiment, Sir Brojendra Lal Mitter, representing the State of Baroda said:[18]

"Sir, this Assembly is framing the Constitution of Free India. We, the states, are an integral part of India and we shall share the freedom with British India. We, therefore, want to share the responsibility of framing the Constitution. (*Hear, hear*).

"We are hereby right of being Indians and not by sufferance. We claim that we are in a position to make substantial contribution to the common task. A hundred and fifty years of unitary British rule has resulted in a measure of uniformity in British India, but in the states there is still a great variety. Some states are as advanced as British India, where the people are associated with the administration. Some are absolute monarchies. Some are feudal and some are primitive. All these have to be fitted into the Indian Constitution, because our 93 millions of population are included in the Indian total of 400 million. We do not want to disturb the main design, as indicated in the first Resolution of this Assembly; but we want to introduce a variety in the pattern so that we may fit into it according to our capacity.

"We want unity in diversity. I appeal to our British Indian colleagues to exercise a little patience with us. We want to march along with them but the pace has to be regulated without impeding the forward move. We are at one with you, in that the Indian Union should be strong in the Centre so that India may hold her head high in the comity of nations. We do not believe in isolated independent existence, which can only weaken the Union. We shall join you wholeheartedly in a spirit of co-operation and not in any spirit of securing special privileges at the cost of the Union. We shall endeavour to make the Constitution develop according to the genius and capacity of the different units, so that the development may be natural and healthy."[18]

Joining the chorus, Sardar K. M. Panikkar, representing the State of Binkaner, said:

"Mr. President, Sir, following what Sir Brojendra Mitter has so very eloquently said, I also, on behalf of the representatives of states who have joined and taken seats today, wish to express our thanks to you, Sir, for the welcome you have extended to us This was indeed the day to which we have been looking forward. It is a dream which has come true, for at no time in India's history has a representative gathering of people who can speak on behalf of the whole of India met and taken counsel. There have been occasions in the past when sections of India have met. We in the states have also been meeting frequently; but never in the history of India, so far as I can remember has there been an occasion when representatives from all parts of India have met together in order to decide their future. Therefore, I consider that the taking of seats of certain representatives of Indian states today has a symbolic value which far outweighs the actual number of representatives who have joined, or the insignificance of members who have themselves joined. This is indeed a symbol of the unity to come and from the work that begins today, in co-operation between the representatives of the states and those of the Indian provinces, we can really hope to look forward to the emergence of a Union of India."[20]

The argument of resting of sovereignty with the state of Jammu & Kashmir arises from the words of the Instrument of Accession:

"8. Nothing in this Instrument affects the continuance of my sovereignty in and over this state, or, save as provided by or under this Instrument, the exercise of any powers, authority and rights now enjoyed by me as a ruler of this state or the validity of any law at present in force in this state."

Since the state government is the successor to the ruler, the state government now possesses sovereignty. There are various problems with this argument. This proceeds on the premise that the state government is the successor of Maharaja's rule. There is no basis to make such an argument. The moment the Constituent Assembly of Jammu & Kashmir completed its functions and adopted democratic institutions the existence of hereditary rulership came to an end. Therefore, once the Constitution of the state came into force, there were no further proclamations/ orders issued by the Maharaja in his capacity as a hereditary ruler.

There is a tendency to refer to the Preamble of the state Constitution to make the point of partial sovereignty of the state. It starts with the words: "We, the people of Jammu & Kashmir". This language is identical to the language of the Preamble of India which starts with "We the people of India". Preamble cannot be interpreted by ignoring the actual words in the operative portions of the Constitution. At the stage when the state was making the Constitution it was expressing that they are an identifiable group. After declaring themselves so, the Constitution goes on to declare that the people have happily agreed to merge themselves into the Union of India. Section 3 of the Jammu & Kashmir Constitution says:

"Section 3: The State of Jammu & Kashmir is and shall be an integral part of the Union of India.

"Further, Section 147 gives a direction that any other provision of the Constitution may be amended, except Section 3, i.e. integration with India."

The effect of all these provisions is that the people of the state have merged their identity with the Union and now the only seat of sovereignty are people of the country as a whole and not people of any state. The Constituent Assembly of Jammu & Kashmir was not unique. Constituent Assemblies of other princely states also did the same thing. They first identified themselves as a group of people and merged their identity with the Union. This procedure was adopted in other princely states as well.[21] Patiala & East Punjab States, Saurashtra, Madhya Bharat, Mysore did adopt the same procedure.

After these declarations by people from princely states, their separate existence and identity got merged into the new country that was legally formed. This was a legal mechanism. Therefore sovereignty rests with the people of India; it cannot rest partially with once state government. The seat of sovereignty with the people of India entirely represents Dr. Ambedkar's concept of India. This vision has no place for sectoral and regional aspirations. India, that is envisaged, is unified and with a strong Centre. The mechanisms devised to create a strong Centre and a peculiar federal structure crafted for India by Dr. Ambedkar are discussed in the following portions of this chapter.

These discussions and the constitutional position in Jammu & Kashmir aptly reflect the vision of Dr. Ambedkar that sovereignty rested with the people of India as a whole and not with some group that claims to be successor of a former princely state was shared by the Constituent Assembly and by the representatives of princely states. All the representatives of princely states, including that of state of Jammu & Kashmir, actively participated in these debates where it was agreed that sovereignty belonged to the entire nation and not to a certain group, as is being alleged by some political groups in Jammu & Kashmir and by the courts in the state. They have ignored the clear statements and commitments made in the Constituent Assembly to this effect. Now arguing that sovereignty is divided and retained in the state of Jammu & Kashmir is disrespect to Dr. Ambedkar, members of the Constituent Assembly and the representatives of Jammu & Kashmir in the Constituent Assembly and the leadership of the state of Jammu & Kashmir that actively accepted and acted, based upon this position.

This position has been confirmed by the Supreme Court in the case of State Bank of India v Santosh Gupta in the following words:

"41. It is rather disturbing to note that various parts of the judgment speak of the absolute sovereign power of the state of Jammu & Kashmir. It is necessary to reiterate that Section 3 of the Constitution of Jammu & Kashmir, which was framed by a Constituent Assembly elected on the basis of universal adult franchise, makes a ringing declaration that the state of Jammu & Kashmir is and shall be an integral part of the Union of India...

"42. It is to be noted that the opening paragraph of the Constitution of India, namely "WE THE PEOPLE OF INDIA, having solemnly resolved to constitute India into a SOVEREIGN SOCIALIST SECULAR DEMOCRATIC REPUBLIC and to secure to all its citizens..." has been wholly omitted in the Constitution of Jammu & Kashmir. There is no reference to sovereignty. Neither is there any use of the expression 'citizen' while referring to its people. The people of Jammu & Kashmir for whom special rights are provided in the Constitution are referred to as "permanent residents" under Part III of the Constitution of Jammu & Kashmir. Above all, the Constitution of Jammu & Kashmir has been made to further define the existing relationship of the state with the Union of India as an integral part thereof.

"43. It is thus clear that the state of Jammu & Kashmir has no vestige of sovereignty outside the Constitution of India and its own Constitution, which is subordinate to the Constitution of India. It is therefore wholly incorrect to describe it as being sovereign in the sense of its residents constituting a separate and distinct class in themselves. ...

"We have been constrained to observe this because in at least three places, the High Court has gone out of its way to refer to a sovereignty which does not exist."[22]

The seat of sovereignty with the people is evidenced in the nature of the Indian federation. Unlike a conventional federation where powers are shared more or less equally between the Centre and the units, Dr. Ambedkar envisaged a strong Centre. A majority of the powers were located with the Centre. This made Centre strong vis-à-vis the units, i.e. states under the Indian Constitution. This arrangement was necessary to foster the feeling of integration in the country and effective administration.

Federation with a Strong Centre

Dr. Ambedkar was aware of the social and political divisions but he constantly spoke about and made effort to bridge the gaps and bring about unity. He understood the practical realities and the basis of differences amongst different groups and the reasons for their demands. But for him, above all such sectoral concerns was national integration and national interest. He emphatically stated in the Constituent Assembly:

"I know today we are divided politically, socially and economically. We are a group of warring camps and I may go even to the extent of confessing that I am probably one of the leaders of such a camp. But, Sir, with all this, I am quite convinced that given time and circumstances, nothing in the world will prevent this country from becoming one. (*applause*) With all our castes and creeds, I have not the slightest hesitation that we shall in some form be a united people (*cheers*)."[23]

Dr. Ambedkar visualised a unified country and was motivated with the objective of creating a strong and a unified nation. He strongly represented the oppressed classes, but never claimed separate national identity for them. He treated them as a part of one nation and extended the same principle to all other segments of society. In his view, there was no place for separate identifies based on region and political identity or background. To achieve this goal, he created a strong a Centre through the Constitution. He openly and candidly supported a "strong united Centre", much stronger than all other prior constitutional arrangements in India.[24] He wanted all differences to fall apart so that India shall become a unified country. A strong Centre could ensure that the differences are taken over by realities of operating political structures.

He achieved this objective through creation of a federation with a strong Centre.

Dr. Ambedkar conceptualised the Constitution of India as federal in nature but unitary in character. India is not strictly a federal state. Nowhere in the Constitution the federal word is used. The idea could have been that using federal could have mellowed down the impact and importance of Union. There were demands raised in the Constituent Assembly to add the word 'federal' so that what was implicit could become explicit.[25] It was thought that the insistence on making implicit explicit should not deprive the Constitution of its strong unitary character. The inclination of Dr. Ambedkar was in favour of a strong Union. He rejected the request to add 'federal' word and the Constituent Assembly joined him in rejecting the suggestion.[26] One of the reasons to insist on use of the word union was to ensure that constituent states do not have the freedom to secede from the union.[27] He repeatedly rejected the request to add 'federation' in place of 'union'.[28]

There are two forms of constitutional structures that define the relationship between the Union and the constituents of the Union, i.e. states. These are: unitary and federation. In the 'unitary' form the Centre or the Union is strong in relation to the constituent units states. The states have very little or no powers as such. United Kingdom is an example of a unitary State. In a federation the states enjoy a great deal of discretion. There are linkages with the Union but the states enjoy a greater degree of freedom in administration. Indian Constitution is defined as a federation with unitary bias.[29] The Constituent Assembly deliberately decided to adopt this unique structure. The choice was practical and aimed at ensuring unity and integrity of the country. They were not interested in using any terminology or a rigid theoretical approach. They were keen to have a strong Centre.[30] Therefore, the word 'federation' is not used anywhere in the Constitution. Article 1 of the Constitution defines India as: "India, that is Bharat, shall be Union of States."

Dr. Ambedkar, carefully, after a thorough thought, described India as a 'Union of States' and not as a 'Federation of States' in Article 1. India is a 'Union of States' created by knitting together the constituent units, but yet it is an undivided and unified entity by itself. India is different from United States where the states come together to form the Centre. In the case of India, the country was already one unit. The units came together under an overarching scheme which had kept them together since the past. Therefore India could not become a conventional federal structure, such as the United States. It always had and continues to possess strong unitary features. Indian Constitution exhibits these characteristics; rather, these characteristics were the method for national unity and integrity through the Constitution.[31] The introduction of these characteristics into the Constitution was an outcome of the efforts of Dr. Ambedkar. There are many more provisions in the Constitution that represent his vision. Over and above the background philosophy for structuring provisions in the Constitution is reflected in the debates in the Constituent Assembly.

The Draft Constitution was criticised for use of 'Union' in place of 'Federation'. Dr. Ambedkar defended the use of 'Union' rather than 'Federation'. According to him, it was not out of place to refer to India as a Union although it was federal in nature. He cited examples of countries where the countries were unitary as well as federal in nature, yet they were called a 'Union'. South Africa is a unitary State and appropriately defined as a Union, but Canada is a federation, still it is called a 'Union'. In Ambedkar's view, "the description of India as a Union, though its Constitution is Federal, does no violence to usage."[32] He was candid to state that "what is important is that the use of the word Union is deliberate."[33] He, thereafter, gave reasons which befittingly describe his vision of the structure of Indian policy:

"I do not know why the word 'Union' was used in the Canadian Constitution, but I can tell you why the Drafting Committee has used it. The Drafting Committee wanted to make it clear that though India was to be a Federation, the Federation was not the result of an agreement by the states to join in a Federation and that the Federation not being the result of an agreement that no State has the right to secede from it. The Federation is a Union because it is indestructible. Though the country and the people may be divided into different states for convenience of administration, the country is one integral whole, its people a single people living under a single *imperium* derived from a single source. The Americans had to wage a civil war to establish that the states have no right of secession and that their Federation was indestructible. The Drafting Committee thought that it was better to make it clear at the outset rather than to leave it to speculation or to dispute."[34]

What flows very clearly from his thinking is that India is not a deliberate creation after entering into an agreement of states. India was and is one. It is not only one, it is indestructibly one. No element that constitutes the Union has a right to secede from India. All units are an integral part of India. For him, they are not only unified in perpetuity but also equal. None of them can claim a 'special status' or 'autonomy'. In relation to Jammu & Kashmir arguments are often raised that Jammu & Kashmir has autonomy[35] or a special status.[35]

Through Article 1, Dr. Ambedkar demolished differences between provinces and princely states. They became equal. Article 1 defines all units of India as 'states', irrespective of whether they were provinces or princely states in past. The use of the word 'states' should not be confused with princely states. The word 'states' destroys the difference between provinces and states. 'States' is used as composite word to represent 'provinces' as well as 'states'. Some members of the Constituent Assembly suggested using different words, most of which were Hindi translations of the state. They argued that words such as 'provinces' or '*pradesh*' may be used. Dr. Ambedkar opposed such suggestions and defended the idea of calling and treating all units uniformly and calling them states. This was accepted by the Constituent Assembly.[37] Furthermore, the list of states defined under Article 1 that constitute units of India are listed in Schedule 1. In this list Jammu & Kashmir appears at serial number 15. By referring to Jammu & Kashmir with a general phrase of 'state' any potential argument of special status was discarded. It is therefore, treated equal to all other states in India, without any special or privileged position.

Dr. Ambedkar strove to create a robust Centre through the Constitution. Pointing out to the practical working of federal constitutions in the world, he said that the Centre was bound to become stronger. He explained the need of a strong Centre for India based on the American experience. In the U.S.A., the government at the Centre, which is known as the Centre of Union Government in India is called the federal government. The units of the federation are called States. In India too, we call the constituent units as states. In the U.S.A. the federal government is given far lesser powers under the American Constitution. Over time, the importance of the Centre has grown and has overshadowed and eclipsed the state governments. This change has come about due to modern conditions.[38] A strong Centre becomes a practical necessity. It introduces uniformity and thereby ease of administration. The Centre acts as a strong centripetal force to ensure that the entire State is held together strongly. In the age of communication where linkages and mobility within the country proliferate it is natural for the Centre to become strong. Dr. Ambedkar carefully drafted the provisions relating to the Indian federal structure. He was aware of the diversity in India. The diversity had to be retained but not at the cost of compromising the unity. To achieve this unity, a strong Centre was necessary. The federal structures of other countries was studied by him. He modified the available models of federalism in other countries to best suit the Indian context.

The federal polity that Dr. Ambedkar devised for India was unique and suitable for the Indian situation. He was aware of the problems with the federal system of the Untied States. Federalism, by nature, is considered to be a weak form of governance. The division of powers between the Centre and states creates two systems in a federal structure. This brings in diversity in the system and makes decision making ineffective. This is felt more acutely in moments of crises. Conventional federal structures, unlike India, aim at prioritising the identities of the regions that the states represent. In the case of India a delicate balance was necessary. There is a possibility that the regional identities get stouter in a federation. There are different laws in each state of a federation. This creates multiple problems for citizens. It becomes difficult to easily travel from one state to another and settle in federal structures like the United States of America. These weaknesses had to be cured for making the Indian Constitution effective.[39] Dr. Ambedkar therefore, devised a peculiar structure for India. He recounted two prominent drawbacks of American federalism.

A federal Constitution normally suffers from two weaknesses: rigidity and legalism. The arduous rigidity is created by the separation of powers and subjects between the federal and the state-level legislatures. A legislature at the Centre/federal level cannot legislate on topics under the coverage of the state level and vice versa. If either indulges in such an activity, then it is unconstitutional. The dispute on whether in fact transgression of powers has taken place or not is decided by the judiciary. The involvement of judiciary in the process is an introduction of legalism.[40] Once judiciary comes into operation, there is ample scope for interpretation. The scope of the powers would then exclusively depend on the interpretation adopted by the courts. It is more informative for courts to decide if the list of subjects is large and clearly specified.

The Indian federalism drafted by Dr. Ambedkar was on the basis of experience of federalism in other countries. The effort was to remove the drawbacks of federalism in those systems and devise a system most efficient and workable for India. In the American system, the nature of federalism was such that the scope of activity for the federal and state governments was rigidly divided. Since a federal Constitution is a written Constitution, further rigidity was introduced. The subjects for the sphere of operation in the U.S.A. are, therefore, strict. One, the federal government cannot legislate on topics within the domain of states and vice versa. If any organ violates the mandate, then the act is unconstitutional and the decision on that would be taken by the Supreme Court. The Supreme Court has had to find out ways of deciding these conflicts by devising various theories. Constitutions framed after the American Constitution have attempted to prune these problems. In Australia, a formula was devised to get over this problem. The Australian Constitution has created a long list for concurrent exercise of jurisdiction. There are a few subjects left for exclusive legislation by the federal legislature, called the Parliament of the Commonwealth. Thus the Parliament of Australia can do many things that American Congress cannot do and if the American Government does so, then it has to persuade the Supreme Court, depending on its "ability, ingenuity and willingness to invent a doctrine to justify its exercise of authority."[41]

The Indian Constitution tackles the problem of rigidity and legalism by adopting a further refined and improved version of federalism as compared to the American and the Australian model. In India, there is a long list of concurrent subjects where both the federal and state legislatures can legislate. But Indian Constitution contemplates a strong Union. It differs from a federal structure to that extent. Therefore, the list of subjects where the Union has exclusive power to legislate is far larger than that of Australia. In the case of Australia only three subjects were reserved exclusively for the Federal Parliament, but in India the Draft Constitution included 91 subjects. Dr. Ambedkar introduced this federal system in the Draft Constitution to achieve "greatest possible flexibility" in a federal system which is "supposed to be rigid by nature."[42]

The other feature of Indian federalism is that it is flexible. Under the American and other federal structures, the federal government cannot interfere at all with the internal administration of states. This is not the case with India. In the case of India, the federal government has the freedom and power to interfere in affairs of states when necessary. On these occasions, the constitutional structure becomes completely unitary. These features are unique to India and no other federation possesses such features.[43] In the ordinary course, the Parliament would legislate on federal subjects. In certain situations, when a subject becomes a matter of national concern, then the Parliament can legislate on all of them.[44] Indian federalism thus gets over the problems of rigidity and legalism. "Its distinguishing feature is that it is a flexible federation."[45] Dr. Ambedkar made it clear that these features are special characteristics of the Indian Constitution and are not found anywhere else.[46]

A federal structure is based on the concept of dual polity. Dual polity means different structures extant at the Central/ provincial level and state level. The authority is divided between these two levels. There is a legislative and executive and judicial powers are separate at these two levels. This creates a lot of diversity, which is understandable to a point. But beyond that, it results in chaos and disruption of the system. This system has produced chaos in different federal states. The American federal system follows dual polity. Dr. Ambedkar specifically distinguished the U.S.A. federal structure from that of India, based on a bond of relationship between the state and the federal government. The association in the case of India is stronger. It is more inclined in favour of a unitary set-up, unlike the federal structure in the U.S.A.. Ambedkar elaborated this distinction as follows:

"The dual polity of the proposed Indian Constitution differs from the dual polity of the U.S.A. in another respect. In the U.S.A. the Constitutions of the federal and the states governments are loosely connected.

In describing the relationship between the Federal and State Government in the U.S.A., Bryce has said:

"The Central or national government and the state governments may be compared to a large building and a set of smaller buildings standing on the same ground, yet distinct from each other."

Distinct they are, but how distinct are the state governments in the U.S.A. from the federal government? Some idea of this distinctness may be obtained from the following facts:

1. Subject to the maintenance of the republican form of government, each state in America is free to make its own Constitution.
2. The people of a state retain forever in their hands, altogether independent of the national government, the power of altering their Constitution.

To put it again in the words of Bryce:

"A state (in America) exists as a commonwealth by virtue of its own Constitution, and all state authorities, legislative, executive and judicial are the creatures of, and subject to the Constitution."[47]

The Indian Constitution achieves uniformity and bridges the differences between them that could be created in a strictly federal structure. There are many linkages that create a strong union. A strong union can ensure that these problems do not arise, as hoped by Dr. Ambedkar and so structured in the Constitution. The structure is such that India is a federation yet there is uniformity in "basic matters which are essential to maintain the unity of the country."[48] Dr. Ambedkar removed the problems associated with a dual polity in the case of India. Explaining this point in the Constituent Assembly, he said:

"A dual judiciary, a duality of legal codes and a duality of civil services, as I said, are the logical consequences of a dual polity which is inherent in a federation. In the U.S.A. the federal judiciary and the state judiciary are separate and independent of each other. The Indian federation, though a dual polity, has no dual judiciary at all. The High Courts and the Supreme Court form one single integrated judiciary having jurisdiction and providing remedies in all cases arising under the constitutional law, the civil law or the criminal law. This is done to eliminate all diversity in all remedial procedures. Canada is the only country which furnishes a close parallel. The Australian system is only an approximation.

"Care is taken to eliminate all diversity from laws which are at the basis of civic and corporate life. The great Codes of Civil & Criminal Laws, such as the Civil Procedure Code, Penal Code, the Criminal Procedure Code, the Evidence Act, Transfer of Property Act, Laws of Marriage, Divorce and Inheritance, are either placed in the Concurrent List so that the necessary uniformity can always be preserved without impairing the federal system.

"The dual polity which is inherent in a federal system as I said is followed in all federations by a dual service. In all federations there is a Federal Civil Service and a State Civil Service. The Indian federation, though a dual polity will have a dual service but with one exception. It is recognised that in every country there are certain posts in its administrative set-up which might be called strategic from the point of view of maintaining the standard of administration. It may not be easy to spot such posts in a large and complicated machinery of administration. But there can be no doubt that the standard of administration depends upon the calibre of the civil servants who are appointed to these strategic posts. Fortunately for us, we have inherited from the past system of administration which is common to the whole of the country and we know what are these strategic posts. The Constitution provides that without depriving the states of their right to form their own civil services, there shall be an All India service recruited on an All India basis with common qualifications, with uniform scale of pay and the members of which alone could be appointed to these strategic posts throughout the Union.

"Such are the special features of the proposed federation."[49]

Dr. Ambedkar introduced a uniform system on crucial factors throughout the country and gave the control of such strategic positions to the Centre. Dr. Ambedkar created multiple institutions which would ensure that the Centre remains strong. The Draft Constitution has sought to forge means and methods whereby India will have uniformity in all basic matters which are essential to maintain the unity of the country. Unification was achieved by putting the Centre in control of three crucial provisions: 1) single judiciary, 2) common All-India Civil Service to man important posts, and 3) uniformity in fundamental laws, civil and criminal.[50]

Explaining the importance of a unified judiciary, he said:

"A dual judiciary, a duality of legal codes and a duality of civil services, as I said, are the logical consequences of a dual polity which is inherent in a federation. In the U.S.A. the federal judiciary and the state judiciary are separate and independent of each other. The Indian federation, though a dual polity, has no dual judiciary at all. The High Courts and the Supreme Court form one single integrated judiciary having jurisdiction and providing remedies in all cases arising under the constitutional law, the civil law or the criminal law. This is done to eliminate all diversity in all remedial procedures. Canada is the only country which furnishes a close parallel. The Australian system is only an approximation."[51]

Jammu & Kashmir deviates on these principles. In

relation to judiciary, for a long time it did not adhere to the jurisdiction of the Supreme Court. Article 136 and 32 of the Indian Constitution were inapplicable to the state.[52]

Duality created due to different domestic laws is problematic. It creates immense practical difficulties for the citizens. Dr Ambedkar summarised this position aptly in the following words:

"One has only to imagine twenty different laws if we have twenty states in the union of marriage, of divorce, of inheritance of property, family relations, contracts, torts, crimes, weights and measures, of bills and cheques, banking and commerce, of procedures for obtaining justice and in the standards and methods of administration. Such a state of affairs not only weakens the state but becomes intolerant to the citizen who moves from state to state only to find that what is lawful in one state is not lawful in another."[53]

Dr. Ambedkar removed these complexities in the Indian system. He achieved uniformity and unity of the Indian federation through commonality of basic laws, especially civil and criminal laws. He elaborated the steps taken for removal of divergences in the following words:

"Care is taken to eliminate all diversity from laws which are at the basis of civic and corporate life. The great Codes of Civil & Criminal Laws, such as the Civil Procedure Code, Penal Code, the Criminal Procedure Code, the Evidence Act, Transfer of Property Act, Laws of Marriage, Divorce and Inheritance, are either placed in the Concurrent List so that the necessary uniformity can always be preserved without impairing the federal system."[54]

This very fundamental principle that Dr. Ambedkar wanted to be a characteristic of India is defeated in the case of Jammu & Kashmir. A cursory glance at most of the statutes would show that they do not apply in the state. Indian Penal Code, which is a criminal law, does not apply in the state. It has a different criminal code, called the Ranbir Penal Code. There are many complications created due to the absence of uniformity in criminal law. A different criminal law applied in Jammu & Kashmir creates practical difficulties. There are many instances that may be discussed but here the focus is only on some prominent provisions. Section 304 B of the Indian Penal Code deals with dowry death. If a woman dies within seven years of her marriage and was subjected to cruelty by the husband or his relatives for demand of dowry, then the death is called dowry death. The presumption is that the husband and his relatives have caused this death. This is an important provision to curtail demands of dowry and harassment of women that has often led to killing of women. This provision is absent in the Ranbir Criminal Code. There will be no presumption of dowry death in the state. If someone takes his wife to Jammu & Kashmir and causes her death within seven years as an outcome of dowry demand, then will such a person be punishable? The Ranbir Penal Code says that a person would not be. These provisions are not only creating dual polity but are discriminating against women. Dr. Ambedkar weaved these provisions in the federal structure to ensure that all parts of the country achieve same levels of social progress. Jammu & Kashmir is left behind in the stream, in contravention of Dr. Ambedkar's vision.

Section 190 A of the Ranbir Penal Code states that the state government can punish anyone which circulates, publishes anything whereof forfeited to the government and the decision whether the material is seditious or not is made by the Chief Minister.

This is a violation of freedom of press as well as the principle of separation of powers. The press is at the mercy of the government; moreover, the Chief Minister performs the judicial function of deciding criminality of a person. The executive performs judicial function. These are archaic provisions which hurt the concept of fundamental rights and freedom of expression that Dr. Ambedkar stipulated in the Indian Constitution.

There are many such instances. The Code of Civil Procedure,

Criminal Procedure, Law of Contract and other business and labour laws are different in the state of Jammu & Kashmir. The efforts of Dr. Ambedkar at curtailing dual polity in India are defeated in Jammu & Kashmir. This has resulted in practical difficulties for residents of Jammu & Kashmir as well as citizens in other parts of India who would like to have closer business association with the state.

An important thread to weave unity was the structure of the administrative services. There were to be state as well as all-India services. The All India service is vital. The key and strategic position has to be occupied by members of a unified service through the All India service. This will also ensure that persons with high calibre to have competed at the national level will be placed at important positions in all the states. Reflecting on the importance of uniformity in relation to the All India service, Dr. Ambedkar said:

"The dual polity which is inherent in a federal system, as I said, is followed in all federations by a dual service. In all federations, there is a Federal Civil Service and a State Civil Service. The Indian federation, though a dual polity, will have a dual service but with one exception. It is recognised that in every country there are certain posts in its administrative set-up which might be called strategic from the point of view of maintaining the standard of administration. It may not be easy to spot such posts in a large and complicated machinery of administration. But there can be no doubt that the standard of administration depends upon the calibre of the civil servants who are appointed to these strategic posts. Fortunately for us, we have inherited from the past system of administration which is common to the whole of the country and we know what are these strategic posts. The Constitution provides that without depriving the states of their right to form their own civil services, there shall be an All India service recruited on an All India basis with common qualifications, with uniform scale of pay and the members of which alone could be appointed to these strategic posts throughout the Union."[55]

In Jammu & Kashmir, constant efforts are made to reduce the appointment of officers from All India service. The State Autonomy Report recommended that Article 312 of the Constitution should be amended to reduce the presence of officers from All India services. The reasons given were:

"Notwithstanding seemingly an attractive proposition, one can say without any fear of contradiction that it has dwarfed local talent and made it difficult for local youth to aspire to compete for key civil posts on competitive basis. The weak-kneed attempt to organise Kashmir Civil Service is neither here nor there and increasing inflow of All India services has meant pretty little in the field for which the services were apparently conceived. No Imperial model of civil services in central cadre can be or could be a substitute for what the local youth could be expected to have i.e. local patriotic feeling and passionate attachment for the service of those among whom they live. Ever since the application of these provisions of the Indian Constitution to our state, the number of direct recruits from the state has been negligible. The problem has attained so unpleasant a shape, even in the national context, that demands of greater number of promotious from local services all over the counhy have assumed alarming proportions."[56]

The reasoning itself is skewed. Furthermore, the Group of Interlocutors for Jammu & Kashmir appointed by the Government of India made similar suggestions. The report made a suggestion that the presence of officers from All India service should be gradually removed from the state of Jammu & Kashmir.[57] It is unfortunate that in Jammu & Kashmir efforts are being made to outrightly defeat the measures that Dr. Ambedkar undertook to keep India together.

Conclusions

Dr. Ambedkar's assessment of his time that the Centre is getting stronger and will get stronger further is established with the turn of events since the drafting of the Constitution. In the modern era of international trade and commerce, it is convenient for a country to stick together and address these challenges. Countries that are able to consolidate them internally are in a far better position to tackle the associated issues of international relations. The negotiating power of the countries is consolidated vis-à-vis other countries. The size of a country is an influential factor. It decides the size of its markets and consumption potential of a country. Therefore countries try to consociate and unify their internal administration. The convergence in the European Union is a prominent example. It is a block of different nations that has come together. Here it is not states; rather, different countries that have come together to derive maximum benefits of the international trading system. It is natural for large countries to converge at a strong Centre. Countries have internally ensured uniformity by creating a single market. The General Sales and Goods Tax to be introduced in India is an effort to create a single and uniform market. Other federal countries, such as Canada and Australia, have already created such strong centralised regimes.

Views expressed by Dr. Ambedkar on federalism and the concept of India with a strong Centre are very crucial. He had successfully translated his views into words. They are expressed after subjecting his views to a complex and difficult drafting exercise. More than that, he had expressed his arguments and tested them with his colleagues in the Drafting Committee before they could become a part of the Draft Constitution.

The concept of India introduced in the Constitution is the one where all states that are constituents of India are equal and all persons residing in different parts of India are equal. The Indian experience from the operation of the Constitution shows that the country has remained together. There have been some instances of efforts to secede from the country, but all the efforts were minor and quelled immediately. No institution in the India polity has claimed a special treatment. Jammu & Kashmir is the only state that has claimed separate constitutional identity. The only reason for these claims is failure to respect Dr. Ambedkar's vision for India and apply it uniformly throughout India. Dr. Ambedkar's vision has proved successful in the entire country, then why should it not applied in Jammu & Kashmir? Rather, its application in Jammu & Kashmir would have ensured that the problems faced in the state would not have arisen. Since they have arisen now, the solution to them lies in applying Dr. Ambedkar's vision to the state immediately. Dr. Ambedkar was a visionary and aware that even if one former princely state is left out of the constitutional regime applied to the rest of India, it would create insurmountable challenges. The country faces this challenge for not applying Dr. Ambedkar's vision in the state of Jammu & Kashmir.

References

1. States means present day states such as Maharashtra, Haryana, Andhra Pradesh, etc. States should not be confused with the princely states discussed in the last chapter
2. *Island of Palmas Case* (Netherlands, U.S.A.), 4 April 1928 (1928), 2 RIAA 829, 838
3. Montevideo Convention
4. Constituent Assembly Debates Official Report (*CAD*), Reprint by Lok Sabha Secretariat, New Delhi (2009) Book 1, 59
5. *CAD*, Book 2, p. 414
6. Ibid
7. Ibid, p. 418
8. Ashok Kumar & Others Vs State of J & K & Others, SWP No. 1290 of 2014, para 36, JK HC
9. Above note 5, Vol . 7, Dr. Ambedkar responding to the debate on Article 1, p. 418
10. Above note 4, Book 1, pp. 271-2
11. Ibid, 272
12. Ibid, p. 128-9
13. Ibid, p. 121
14. Ibid, p. 142
15. Ibid, pp. 128-9
16. Ibid, p. 317
17. Ibid, p. 320

18. Above note 4
19. Ibid, p. 367
20. Ibid, p. 367- 8
21. *CAD*, Book 5 (12 October, 1949). For details, *see* speech by Sardar Patel in the Constituent Assembly
22. Bank of India v. Santosh Gupta, Civil Appeal Nos. 12237-12238 of 2016
23. Above note 4, p. 100
24. Ibid, p. 103
25. Above note 5, speech of KT Shah, p. 400
26. Ibid, p. 403
27. Ibid
28. Ibid, p. 404
29. DD Basu's commentary on the Constitution of India, *Introduction to the Constitution of India*, Vol. I, 8th edn, Wadhwa and Company, 2007, pp. 51-6
30. Granville Austin, *The Indian Constitution: Cornerstone of a Nation* (OUP, 1999), pp. 231-2
31. Ibid, p. 12
32. Above note 5, p. 33
33. Ibid
34. Ibid
35. *See State Autonomy Committee Report*. The report is primarily a document created by a political party. It may be a political manifesto, but it hardly possesses any constitutional or legal value. Other commentators fall in the mistaken belief that the state is autonomous. The committee appointed under the Chairmanship of Padgaonkar also came to the same conclusions that the State has autonomy, which has been taken away and needs to be restored
36. Recent decisions of J.K. High Court: Parimoksh Seth vs. State of J & K and others, Prof. S.M. Iqbal Qadri vs. State of J & K and others (Beef Ban verdict), Ashok Kumar and others vs. State of J & K and others (9 October, 2015), Bhupinder Singh Sodhi vs. Union of India and Santosh Gupta vs. Union of India. (16 July, 2015)
37. *CAD*, Book 4, pp. 403-12
38. Above note 5, p. 42
39. Ibid, p. 34
40. Ibid, p. 35

41. Ibid, p. 35
42. Ibid, pp. 35-6
43. Ibid, Speech of Dr. Ambedkar, p. 34-5
44. Ibid, p. 36
45. Ibid.
46. Ibid.
47. Ibid, p. 34
48. Ibid, p. 36-37
49. Ibid.
50. Ibid.
51. Ibid.
52. Art. 136 applied on J & K after 20 Jan, 1960 and Art. 32, Cl. (3) is still not applicable there, for details *see* C.O 1954
53. Above note 5, p. 36
54. Ibid, p. 37
55 Ibid
56. Report of the State Autonomy Committee, adopted by the State Legislative Assembly on June 26, 2000 & by the State Legislative Council on June 27, 2000 in a special session, pp. 116-117
57. Report of Interlocutors for Jammu & Kashmir: A New Compact with the People of Jammu & Kashmir, Final Report, Dileep Padgaonkar, Radha Kumari, M.M. Ansari (2012), p. 5

4

Ambedkar and Article 370

The last two chapters discussed Dr. Ambedkar's vision for India: a federal structure with a strong Centre. Dr. Ambedkar was particularly keen that all the constituents of India, whether they have been provinces or princely states under British, are equal under the new Constitution. The wedge between the provinces and princely states had existed for over a century and it was a challenge to bridge the gap between the two. Dr. Ambedkar successfully achieved the task by crafting the Constitution in such a manner that antecedent differences would vanish and be replaced by a uniform framework, representing equality between former provinces and princely states. The present situation of units of the Indian Union – between themselves – and between the Centre and states represents success of his vision and the steps he took under the Indian Constitution to achieve that vision.

It is only one former princely state in which his vision was not realised, although a democratically elected government came in place of the former hereditary rule. This is the state of Jammu & Kashmir. The fundamental reason for the different and often special treatment claimed is Article 370. This chapter looks at the manner in which Article 370 was created and incorporated in the Constitution and how it conflicts with Dr. Ambedkar's vision of India.

Genesis of Article 370

Article 370 was introduced in the Constituent Assembly as Draft Article 306-A by Gopalaswamy Ayyangar on 17 October 1949. In his speech he elucidated the essential features of Article 370. Article 370 was introduced to facilitate the application of provisions of the Indian Constitution - in addition to Article 1 and Article 370 which were automatically applicable—till the time the Constituent Assembly of the state was convened. Once a Constituent Assembly was convened in Jammu & Kashmir and it performed its functions, Article 370 became unnecessary and had to be removed. As was discussed in Chapter 2, in princely states, after the ruler had signed the Instrument of Accession, Constituent Assembly was to be constituted in the state that would pass a resolution endorsing the integration of the state into India. This Constituent Assembly was to also endorse and accept the Constitution of India drafted by the Constituent Assembly, applicable to India as well as the states and defining the relationship between the Union and the states.

There was resistance to incorporation of Article 370 by some members of the Constituent Assembly. Maulana Hasarat Mohani found this provision discriminatory and questioned why a different treatment was given to Jammu & Kashmir and it was not being treated same as other princely states. N. Gopalaswami Ayyangar promised the Constituent Assembly that Article 370 (Draft Article 306-A) was only a temporary provision. He said:

"Now, if you remember the viewpoints that I have mentioned, it is an inevitable conclusion that, at the present moment, we could establish only an interim system. Article 306 A is an attempt to establish such a system."[1] (emphasis added)

N. Gopalaswami Ayyangar stated that this was being done due to the peculiar situation in the state. He explained:

"The discrimination is due to special conditions of Kashmir. That particular state is not yet ripe for this kind of integration. It is the hope of everybody here that in due course even Jammu & Kashmir will become ripe for the same sort of integration as has taken place in the case of other states. (*Cheers*) At present it is not possible to achieve that integration. There are various reasons why this is not possible now, I shall refer again to this a little later."[2]

The need to make a temporary provision arose in Jammu & Kashmir due to the peculiar circumstances existing in the state. The territory was attacked and some parts of the territory were under foreign control. There was a cease-fire agreed at the United Nations. Until the situation became normal, it was not possible to convene a Constituent Assembly. Explaining this situation, N. Gopalaswami Ayyangar said:

"I do not want to take much of the time of the House, but I shall briefly indicate what the special conditions are. In the first place, there has been a war going on within the limits of Jammu & Kashmir state.

"There was cease-fire agreed to at the beginning of this year and that cease-fire is still on. But the conditions in the state are still unusual and abnormal. They have not settled down. It is therefore necessary that the administration of the state should be geared to these unusual conditions until normal life is restored as in the case of the other states.

"Part of the state is still in the hands of rebels and enemies.

"We are entangled with the United Nations in regard to Jammu & Kashmir and it is not possible to say now when we shall be free from this entanglement."[3]

N. Gopalaswami Ayyanger gave an assurance to the Constituent Assembly that Article 370 was only a temporary arrangement and once Constituent Assembly was formed in the state and performed its functions, Article 370 would be unnecessary. Stating the genesis of Article 370, N. Gopalaswami Ayyengar said:

"Till a Constituent Assembly comes into being, only an interim arrangement is possible and not an arrangement which could at once be brought into line with the arrangements that exists in the case of the other states."[4]

Article 370 was not meant to grant a special status to Jammu & Kashmir. It was made clear that although the Instrument of Accession took place on the basis of four subjects: defence, external affairs, communication and entries related to these subjects, since by the creation of the Indian Constitution with the participation of representatives of princely states, the relationship between the Centre and the state would be regulated by the new Constitution. The Constitution of India regulates the relationship between Jammu & Kashmir and the Centre and the limited relationship contemplated by the Instrument of Accession was inapplicable. Elucidating this scheme N. Gopalaswami Ayyangar stated in the Constituent Assembly:

"As the House is also aware, Instrument of Accession will be a thing of past in the new Constitution. The states have been integrated with the federal republic in such a manner that they do not have to accede or execute a document of accession for the purpose of becoming units of the republic, but they are mentioned in the Constitution itself; and, in the case of practically, all states other that the state of Jammu & Kashmir, their constitutions also have been embodied in the Constitution for the whole of India. All those other states have agreed to integrate themselves in that way and accept the Constitution provided."[5]

This was acceptable to the ruler of Jammu & Kashmir. The ruler of Jammu & Kashmir issued a Proclamation on 25 November 1949. In the proclamation, the Constitution of India was accepted and it was further stated that the Constitution would regulate the relationship of the Centre with the state and replace all pre-existing arrangements. The relationship between Dominion of India and the state of Jammu & Kashmir was regulated through the Instrument of Accession, governed by the Government of India Act, 1935. This arrangement was replaced by the Constitution. The relevant portion of Proclamation of 25 November 1949 is:

"WHEREAS with the inauguration of the new Constitution for the whole of India now being framed by the Constituent Assembly of India, the Government of India Act, 1935, which now governs the constitutional relationship between this state and the Dominion of India will stand repealed;

"AND WHEREAS, in the best interests of this state, which is closely linked with the rest of India by a community of interests in the economic, political and other fields, it is desirable that the constitutional relationship established between this state and the contemplated Union of India and the Constitution of India as drafted by the Constituent Assembly of India, which includes duly appointed representatives of this state, provides a suitable basis for doing so."[6]

The Indian Constitution was to be extended to Jammu & Kashmir in the meanwhile, subject to exceptions and modifications. This limitation on extending the Indian Constitution was only for a temporary period and considering "particular conditions of Jammu & Kashmir." N. Gopalaswami Ayyangar informed the Constituent Assembly that it was not the intention of the government of Jammu & Kashmir that the provisions of the Constitution of India were not to apply to Jammu & Kashmir.[7]

Article 370 imposed an additional procedure for application of the Constitution of India and certain laws made by Parliament to Jammu & Kashmir, until the time the Constituent Assembly of Jammu & Kashmir finished its functions. Summarising the intention for insertion of Article 370, N. Gopalaswami Ayyangar concluded his speech in the Constituent Assembly by stating:

"The effect of this Article is that the Jammu & Kashmir state which is now part of India will continue to be a part of India, which will be a unit of the future Federal Republic of India and the Union Legislature will get jurisdiction to enact laws on matters specified either in the Instrument of Accession or by later addition with the concurrence of the government of the state."[8]

Nature and Analysis of Article 370

Article 370 which falls in Part XXI of the Constitution, is called 'Temporary, Transitional and Special Provisions.' The original title of Part XXI was 'Temporary and Transitional Provisions'. Then, the part contained only three provisions—Articles 369, 370 and Article 371. Article 369 is a transitional provision and Article 370 is a temporary provision. The word 'special' was added by the Constitution (Thirteenth Amendment) Act, 1962, which came into effect on 1 December 1963. The word 'special' was applied only to cover Articles 371 A to I that were inserted in the Constitution through the Constitution (Thirteenth Amendment) Act, 1962. The Statement of Objects and Reasons of Constitution (Thirteenth Amendment) Act, 1962 states:

"In July, 1960, an agreement was reached by the Government of India with the leaders of the Naga People's Convention under which it was decided that Naga Hills-Tuensang Area (Nagaland), which is at present a Part 'B' tribal area within the state of Assam, will be formed into a separate state in the Union of India."

The title of Article 370 is: 'Temporary Provisions with Respect to the State of Jammu & Kashmir". A title plays an important role in interpretation of a constitutional provision.[9] The title makes it abundantly clear that Article 370 is a temporary provision.

Article 370 contemplates that irrespective of the provisions of the Indian Constitution, the provisions contained in Article 370 will be applicable to Jammu & Kashmir. Article 370 provides that the provisions of Article 238 would not apply to Jammu & Kashmir.[10] Article 238 retained the distinction between Part A, Part B and Part C and which was removed with the State Reorganisation Act, 1956. This provision was anyway inapplicable to Jammu & Kashmir because the state had a large area and a complete territorial unit. It was not required to be grouped with other territories to form a viable administrative unit.[11]

Article 370 (1) (b) and (c) relate to application of laws made by Parliament and provisions of the Constitution to Jammu & Kashmir respectively. Article 370 (1) (b) limits the power of Parliament to make laws. The Parliament can make laws on subjects listed in the Union List and State List of the Seventh Schedule. (This topic is discussed in detail in Chapter 6). Article 370 (1) (b) limits the power of Parliament to make laws in relation to Jammu & Kashmir. If the Parliament is making laws on any of the subjects that were a part of the annexure to the Instrument of Accession: defence, external affairs, communication and related subjects in 'consultations' with the state government of Jammu & Kashmir. For laws made on any other subject covered in the Union or Concurrent List, 'concurrence' of the state government of Jammu & Kashmir is necessary. As the words suggest, 'consultation' involves a process of taking into account the opinion of the state government. The opinion of the state government is not binding, whereas 'concurrence' suggests that the state government should agree to application of laws. An awkward situation is created due to continuation of Article 370 even after its originally stipulated objective. When the Parliament makes laws, it has representatives from Jammu & Kashmir in both Lok Sabha and Rajya Sabha. Therefore, the representatives of Jammu & Kashmir are involved in the law-making process in the Parliament like any other state. Seeking another round of 'consultation' or 'concurrence' after the law is passed by Parliament is unnecessary. It gives scope to the state government to block certain welfare legislations which do not suit the part in power in the state.

The Constituent Assembly was promised that the power

of the Parliament was limited in relation to Jammu & Kashmir, only as a temporary provision. This provision, created only to serve under Constituent Assembly, was formed in sate of Jammu & Kashmir. N. Gopalaswamy Ayyangar said in the Constituent Assembly:

"Clause (b) (ii) refers to possible additions to the list in the Instrument of Accession and these additions could be made according to the provisions of this Article with the concurrence of the government of the state. The idea is that even before the Constituent Assembly meets, it may be necessary in the interests of both the Centre and state that certain items which are not included in the Instrument of Accession would be appropriately added to the list in that Instrument so that administration, legislation ad executive action might be furthered, and as this may happen before the Constituent Assembly meets, the only authority from whom we can get consent for the addition is the government of the state. That is provided for."

The explanation to Article 370 (1) (b) recognises the continuation of monarchy. The Constituent Assembly that was staunchly opposed to rulers retaining powers agreed to such an explanation since it was only a temporary provision, until India became a republic. Once India became a republic, there was no scope for any undemocratic and hereditary systems to continue.

Article 370 (1) (d) relates to extension of other provisions of the Constitution in addition to Article 1 and Article 370 which automatically apply. The freedom to apply provisions of the Constitution is given to the President. The President may apply the provisions of the Indian Constitution to the State of Jammu & Kashmir "subject to such exceptions and modifications as the President may by order specify." While applying provisions of the Constitution through an order, the President is required to 'consult' the state government of Jammu & Kashmir if the constitutional provision relates to subjects appended to the Instrument of Accession: defence, external affairs, communication and associated subjects. The President has to obtain 'concurrence' of the state government before applying any other provision.

Thus Article 370 (1) (d) allows the President to interfere with the constitutional scheme. The unfortunate fact is that the President has from time to time interfered and misused and abused this power to stifle the essence of the Constitution. Some fundamental changes effected in the Constitution that destroy the vision of Dr. Ambedkar are discussed in detail in Chapters 5 to 7.

Article 370 (1) (c) is a very important provision. This provision is declaratory that Jammu & Kashmir is an integral part of India. Article 1 applies to Jammu & Kashmir, whether or not Article 370 exists.

Explaining the thinking underlying Article 370 (1) (c) and (d), N. Gopalaswami Ayyangar stated:

"Clauses (c) and (d) refer to the provisions of the Constitution other than the matters listed in Lists I and III. These various provisions have been divided into certain categories. The first, according to this draft is that Article 1 of the Constitution will automatically apply. As we know, it describes the territory of India, and includes amongst these territories all the states mentioned in Part III. With regard to the other provisions in the Constitution, these will apply to Jammu & Kashmir state with success, exceptions and modifications as may be decided on when the President issues an order to that effect. That order can be issued in regard to subjects mentioned in the Instrument of Accession only after consultation with the government of the state. In regard to other matters, the concurrence of that government has to be taken

"Now, it is not the case, nor is the intention of the members of the Kashmir government whom I took the opportunity of consulting before this draft was finalised

– it is not their intention that the other provisions of the Constitution are applied. Their particular point of view is that these provisions should apply only in cases where they can apply the subject to such modifications or exceptions as the particular conditions of the Jammu & Kashmir state may require. I wish to say no more about that particular point at the present moment."[12]

Article 370 (2) states that if the legislation by Parliament and application of the Constitution is done under Article 370 (1) (b) and (c) respectively before the Constituent Assembly was formed in Jammu & Kashmir, then all such decisions shall be put before the Constituent Assembly. This provision enforces the argument that Article 370 was meant to exist only until the Constituent Assembly of Jammu & Kashmir performed its functions. Article 370 only provides for a situation that powers under Article 370 (1) (b) and (c) are exercised prior to the formation of the Constituent Assembly. It does not allow the state government to continue giving 'concurrence' or 'consultation' after the Constituent Assembly is dissolved.

Article 370 (3) provides on of the methods for removal of Article 370. It states: "The President may, by public notification, declare that this Article shall cease to be operative or shall be operative only with such exceptions and modifications and from such date as he may specify." Before the President issues such a notification, recommendation of the Constituent Assembly is necessary.

The text of the Article reflects the intention of the drafters that Article 370 limits the full-fledged application of the entire Constitution of India to Jammu & Kashmir. The moment Article 370 is removed, the entire Constitution of India would be applicable to Jammu & Kashmir. Thus, Article 370 is a temporary provision that was meant to perform two functions until the time the Constituent Assembly in the state of Jammu & Kashmir performed its functions: extension of provisions of the Indian Constitution and extension of laws passed by the Parliament.

Ambedkar and Article 370

Article 370 was not a part of the Constitution of India as drafted by the Constituent Assembly under the leadership of Dr. Ambedkar. Article 370 was added subsequently in the form of Draft Article 306-A. It was discussed as the last provision of the Constitution before the Preamble was taken up for discussion.

Insertion of Article 370 in the Constitution was dramatic. Article 370 was discussed as the last Article before the Preamble was discussed. Dr. Ambedkar did not introduce the provision; N. Gopalswami Ayyangar introduced it. It was an aberration from the procedure as well. Being the Chairman of the Drafting Committee, it was the duty of Dr. Ambedkar to introduce the provisions of the Constitution and respond the debate on the provisions.

The discussion in the preceding chapters, especially in the first chapter, has amply demonstrated the role played by Dr. Ambedkar in the drafting of the Constitution and his involvement in the entire constitution making process. From the debates in the Constituent Assembly, there is one debate where Dr. Ambedkar is conspicuously missed. This debate was on Article 370; Dr. Ambedkar was silent during the debate.

Dr. Ambedkar was aloof from the process of drafting and presentation of Article 370 before the Constituent Assembly. He introduced all other provisions of the Constitution and actively participated in the ensuing debates. He controlled those debates and responded to them and often based on his responses, the fate of the proposed amendments and the shape of the Constitution depended. In the case of Article 370, the provision was neither presented by Dr. Ambedkar nor defended by him. He uttered not a single word during the debate that took place. This was uncharacteristic of his personality. Considering the constitutional function of Chairman of the Drafting Committee that he performed dutifully while other provisions of the Constitution was being discussed was absent during the presentation of Article 370. His silence reflects his resentment towards the provision. He could not have actively voiced his opposition since he was an office bearer in the Constitution-making process, albeit holder of a key position.

He did not support the provision. He could not have opposed the provision, considerating his situation. He was heading the Drafting Committee and it would not have been appropriate for him to oppose the insertion of the provision, while he was holding the constitutional position. He could have objected to the insertion of the provision expressly during the debates, but in that case he would be expected to resign from his position. Moreover, the authors of Article 370 had promised the Constituent Assembly that the provision was temporary and would be removed soon. Once it came to the notice of Dr. Ambedkar that the entire issue of Jammu & Kashmir was being mishandled, he resigned from the government within a year on 27 September 1951. Jammu & Kashmir was one of the important reasons for his resignation and in the letter of resignation he raised this point.

Dr. Ambedkar was opposed to the introduction of Article 370 because that would create a feeling of alienation.[13] No state had a distinct position in the constitutional scheme envisioned by him. The spirit of unification and equality drove him between states and provinces. He expressed his frustration over the manner in which Jammu & Kashmir was handled after its integration into India. His anxiety, generated due to the mishandling of the subject, was one of the reasons for his resignation from the Cabinet on 10 October 1951. His concern was that the Hindus and Buddhists in the state should not be dragged to join Pakistan merely because there is a majority of Muslim population in the state. He was "deeply disturbed" with the foreign policy that India adopted in the case of Jammu & Kashmir.[14]

Consequences of Article 370

Article 370 has resulted in multiple anomalies. These anomalies defeat the vision of Dr. Ambedkar contained in the Constitution of India. There are various steps taken under Article 370 after the Constitution was drafted to defeat the very fundamental provisions provided for in the Constitution by Dr. Ambedkar. The specific unconstitutional actions that defeat his vision are discussed in the following chapters.

Article 370 was created exclusively to tackle the situation in Jammu & Kashmir to serve a limited purpose until the Constituent Assembly of Jammu & Kashmir performed its functions. Despite the Constituent Assembly having finished its job, Article 370 has been continued. Problems have arisen due to wrongful continuation of Article 370. The wrongful continuation goes against the spirit and essence of the Indian Constitution. The assurance to the Constituent Assembly was that Article 370 would not continue after the Constituent Assembly of Jammu & Kashmir finished its work. The continuation of Article 370 despite the completion of the task by the Constituent Assembly of Jammu & Kashmir on 17 November 1956 is a breach of the promise made to the Constituent Assembly and amounts to deceiving Dr. Ambedkar.

It shall be kept in mind that Article 370 had no correlation to the fact of the state of Jammu & Kashmir drafting a separate Constitution. The discussion above shows that all formerly princely states were given this freedom. Despite this freedom, they all decided not to draft a separate state Constitution and allowed a common Constitution to be drafted by the Vellodi Committee. Jammu & Kashmir proceeded to draft a state Constitution. The state Constitution is limited to internal administration of state. It does not compete with the Constitution of India. It is subservient to the Indian Constitution. It was expressly understood that the freedom given to the former princely states to frame constitutions had to operate within a framework. They constituted distinct territorial units but did not possess independent territorial identity. Territorial units that were formerly part of princely states were allowed to frame their own Constitution. But this did not allow them to adopt a distinct framework than the Indian Constitution. The state constitutions had to fall within the framework of the Indian Constitution. In true spirit the so-called state constitutions were actually documents for internal administration rather than a Constitution *per se*. These constitutions were different in nature, purport and content as compared to the constitutions in the states of the U.S.A.. The states there enjoy a far more discretion and are not required to adhere to a framework identified by the federal government. That was not the scheme adopted in India. The framework within which the state Constitution was to be drafted was set out clearly in detail and advance.

More than the manner of introduction of Article 370, the issues of concern are the unconstitutional actions done through abuse of Article 370. Unconstitutional action that are sought to be justified under the cloak of Article 370 contradict Dr. Ambedkar's vision at each stage. Each violation has made the republic of India weak and fundamental rights of people are crushed. Unconstitutional actions that have been undertaken behind the veil of Article 370 are discussed in the following chapters.

References

1. Constituent Assembly Debates Official Report (*CAD*) Reprint by Lok Sabha Secretariat, New Delhi (2009), Book 5, p. 495
2. Ibid, Vol. 10, p. 424
3. Ibid
4. Ibid, p. 425
5. Ibid, pp. 4, 23-24

6. *Legal Documents on Jammu & Kashmir*, Jammu & Kashmir Study Centre 2nd edition, Delhi (2015), p. 67
7. Above note 1, p. 426
8. Ibid, p. 427
9. S. R. Bommai vs. Union of India (1994), 3 SCC 1
10. Constitution of India, Article 370 (1) (a)
11. Government of India, Ministry of States, White Paper on Indian States, The Manager of Publications, Delhi; 1950, Part XI, p. 114
12. Above note 1, p. 426
13. Kuldeep Chand Agnihotri, *Babasaheb Ambedkar – The Troubleshooter Jammu & Kashmir Missed!* (Part I)' available at:http://aseema.net.in/babasaheb-ambedkar-the-troubleshooter-jammu-kashmir-missed-part-1/.
14. Text of the Resignation, *Ambedkar's Writings*, Vol. 14, Part Two, pp.1317-27

❐

5

Separation of Powers and Jammu & Kashmir

Democracy is fundamentally a system of governance run with the wishes of the people. The structures and institutions that operate to run a democratic framework differ vastly. In these frameworks, the manner of participation of the people differs. The nature of the institutions, their powers and interaction is vastly different. Therefore, although United Kingdom, U.S.A and France have democracy, their structures of governance are different. The structures are so dissimilar to each other that they are almost different forms of governance. Structure for governance adopted and applied in whichever form is crucial. Government is an impersonal agency. It is not a human. It operates through its organs or branches. The scope of powers and functions of the organs and branches ultimately decides the nature of democracy. There are three official organs of government constitutionally recognised: legislature, executive and judiciary. The interface between these three organs differs from one democracy to another.

Legislature comprises representatives of the people elected directly or indirectly by the people. Legislature performs the function of law making and ensuring accountability of the executive. In India, it is the Parliament. According to the Constitution, the Parliament comprises "the

President and two Houses to be known respectively as the Council of States and the House of the People".[1] The Council of States is conventionally called 'Rajya Sabha' and comprises of indirectly elected people's representatives from the units of Union: the states.[2] Rajya Sabha ensures that the interests of states are adequately represented and protected at the Centre. The House of the People is conventionally called 'Lok Sabha', which comprises representatives of people elected directly through universal adult suffrage.[3]

The executive is responsible for the execution and implementation of legislations. The head of the executive comprises the President and Council of Ministers headed by the Prime Minister. Although the executive power vests with the President of India,[4] the powers are only symbolic. The executive operates through the Council of Ministers. The members of Council of Ministers are Members of Parliament and accountable to the Parliament. Therefore, when the President is performing executive functions, the powers are, in practice, exercised by the Council of Ministers with the Prime Minister at its helm.

The third limb is the judiciary.[5] The principal task of judiciary is of adjudication. Judiciary is responsible for interpretation of laws and administration of justice. The responsibility of the judiciary is to protect and uphold the constitutional values, especially the rights of citizens against abuse or wrongful exercise of power by the Parliament and executive.[6] It decides whether the law passed by the Parliament is contrary to the Constitution. If it finds so, then the law passed by the Parliament will be declared unconstitutional. Thus, the law would become invalid and lose its force. The judiciary also ensures that the executive is performing its part properly by enforcing laws in their right spirit and within the framework of the Constitution.

The Constitution creates these institutions and specifies the extent of powers they can exercise under the Constitution. Their territories are earmarked and one institution cannot interfere in the activities of another institution. This principle is called separation of powers.[7] The separation of powers ensures that one limb does not interfere in the sphere of activity of another.[8] There is a balance in the system introduced by separation of powers. If one limb oversteps its powers and ventures into the powers exercised by another limb, then such an action is unconstitutional.

In the American constitutional system, the separation of powers is absolute. There is no direct relationship between the three limbs. Only limited interaction between the wings of government is permitted. All the limbs are independent from one another and one person cannot be a part of more than one institution. In India the three organs of government are interlinked. They are interlinked in such a manner that one exerts control over another through a system of internal check and balance. Despite the interlinking, one branch cannot take over another or interfere in the affairs of another. We adopt separation of powers to the extent that one branch shall not overstep its limitations and enter into the domain of another branch.[9] The division of powers between the three organs is not strictly demarcated, yet there is acknowledgement of limits of activity for each branch. There may be some overlap, but the areas of activity are sufficiently differentiated.[10] Hence, "The Court cannot arrogate to itself any function which is left to the domain of the other two branches, namely, the executive and the legislature."[11] Likewise, executive cannot venture into the domain of legislature and judiciary. According to the Supreme Court, "The doctrine of separation of powers is founded on the incapacity of one government department to receive or exercise the powers of the other two."[12] They have to exercise their powers withtin the functions allotted to them by the Constitution.[13] Separation of powers is a basic feature of the Constitution.[14] Basic features of the Constitution are those which are permanent and cannot be changed by Parliament. Interfering with the basic features would amount to destroying the foundations of the Constitution. Therefore, the executive, i.e. the President working under the advice of the Prime Minister and Council of Ministers, cannot make laws and change the Constitution. These powers rest exclusively with the Parliament and only the Parliament can perform these tasks.

Dr. Ambedkar had a specific and clear vision about the institution, the scope of their powers and separation of powers between these institutions. The domain of their operations was specified and limitations were imposed on their sphere of operation to ensure that they do not overstep into the territory of one another. These institutional structures were installed keeping in mind the practicalities of administration. Moreover, they were instituted to foster democratic spirit with people's participation. An important institution in the structure is the Parliament, which has a prominent role because Dr. Ambedkar envisaged a parliamentary democracy. In the Indian parliamentary democracy, which is inspired by the British model, the executive is responsible to the Parliament.

Ambedkar's Vision of Parliamentary Democracy

Dr. Ambedkar envisioned a system of parliamentary democracy for India. Parliament is the forum for expression of the wishes and expectations of the people. Through their representatives, the Parliament is expected to serve, people directly and effectively.

The Constitution is supreme and divides powers between the three organs. There is an inherent bent in favour of the Parliament in the Constitution. Therefore the democracy Dr. Ambedkar introduced for India is parliamentary democracy. Influence of Dr. Ambedkar in making India a parliamentary democracy is evident. The responsibility of deciding the institutional structure for governance under the Constitution was left entirely for the Drafting Committee which was headed by him. When the discussion commenced in the Constituent Assembly, the first task undertaken was to a pass the Resolution on Aims and Objectives. This resolution set out a broad vision for the Constitution, such as democracy, people's participation and equality between princely states and provinces. Details were not mentioned. The task of determining details was given to the Drafting Committee. Accordingly, the Drafting Committee worked out the detailed structures and Dr. Ambedkar proposed and supported these structures in the Constituent Assembly.

Initiating the debate on the Draft Constitution in the Constituent Assembly, Dr. Ambedkar set out his vision for the 'kind of government' that India would apply for the future. He said:

"Turning to the main question, a student of Constitutional Law, if a copy of a Constitution is placed in his hands, is sure to ask two questions. Firstly what is the form of government that is envisaged in the Constitution; and secondly, what in the form of the Constitution? For these are the two crucial matters which every Constitution has to deal with. I will begin with the first of the two questions.

"In the Draft Constitution there is placed at the head of the Indian Union a functionary who is called the President of the Union. The title of this functionary reminds one of the President of the United States. But beyond identity of names, there is nothing in common between the forms of government prevalent in America and the form of government proposed under the Draft Constitution. The American form of government is called the Presidential system of government. What the Draft Constitution proposes is the parliamentary system. The two are fundamentally different."[15]

Constitutionally, Parliament performs the important task of legislation, i.e. making laws. There are two aspects of the power of the Parliament: legislative power and constituent power.

The Parliament enjoys extensive powers in its capacity as a body holding constituent power. In this capacity the Parliament exercises the powers to amend the Constitution. In the words of the Supreme Court, the power of the Parliament to amend the Constitution under Article 368 is "sui generis and cannot be compared to the law-making power of Parliament."[16] It is higher than the ordinary law-making power; it is a sovereign power and subject to the Constitution. It is all embracing and includes not only legislative but also executive and judicial powers within its ambit.[17] While exercising constituent power, the Parliament is operating as a sovereign power and not as an organ created under the Constitution.[18] The limitation on constituent power is that it does not become the original Constituent Assembly and is subject to control of the Parliament.[19]

Legislative power is a subsidiary power that flows from the Constitution. This power gives authority to the Parliament to make laws. These laws have to fall within the contours of the Constitution. The difference between the constituent power and the legislative power is that while operating as a legislative power, it has to function within the limitations of the Constitution. The laws made by the Parliament cannot contradict the constitutional provisions. However, while acting as a constituent power, the Parliament can amend the Constitution itself. This in a way is the power to change the rules of the game. Therefore, if the Parliament cannot make some laws because they would contradict the Constitution, the Parliament can amend the Constitution and then make the law, which would be then legal and valid. The constituent power of the Parliament to amend the Constitution is not uncontrolled. It is controlled by the basic structure of the doctrine laid down in the case of Kesvananda Bharti vs. Union of India. As per the basic structure doctrine, there are certain foundational principles that cannot be amended by the Parliament, except these limitations, the powers of the Parliament to amend the Constitution are unlimited. Therefore, in India, we have adopted the principle of parliamentary sovereignty. Parliamentary sovereignty is different from parliamentary supremacy. United Kingdom follows Parliamentary supremacy: Parliament is higher in comparison to other institutions. In the case of India, only the Constitution is higher in comparison to all limbs of the government. Within the limitations of the Constitution, the Parliament is sovereign. Indian Constitution is aptly described by Jennings as "sovereign within its powers".[20] Parliament enjoys plenary powers within the sphere of their competence.[21]

Being a parliamentary democracy, there is a bent in favour of powers to the Parliament. This is appropriate since Parliament is the body containing representatives of people elected by the people. In parliamentary democracy, the executive is accountable to the Parliament. The members of the Council of Ministers, i.e. the executive are members of the Parliament. The executive remains in power only until they enjoy a majority in the Parliament. The President is only a titular head and the actual governance is done by the Council of Ministers, headed by the Prime Minister. The Council of Ministers governs under the name of the President but is in fact accountable to the Parliament. There is no accountability of Council of Ministers towards the President. Therefore, the system is parliamentary democracy. Dr. Ambedkar distinguished the Indian democracy from the American democracy by providing that the executive remains accountable to the Parliament and not free to operate on its own or accountable to the President. The President of India is only similar to the President of the U.S.A. in name. Their powers are vastly different. The President is only a titular head. Explaining this system, Dr. Ambedkar stated in the Constituent Assembly:

"The presidential system of America is based upon the separation of the executive and the legislature, so that the President and his secretaries cannot be members of the Congress. The Draft Constitution does not recognise this doctrine. The ministers under the Indian Union are members of Parliament. Only Members of Parliament can become ministers. Ministers have the same rights as other members of Parliament, namely, that they can sit in Parliament, take part in debates and vote in its proceedings. Both systems of government are of course democratic and the choice between the two is not very easy. A democratic executive must satisfy two conditions : (1) It must be a stable executive and (2) it must be a responsible executive. Unfortunately, it has not been possible so far to devise a system which can ensure both in equal degree. You can have a system which can give you more stability but less responsibility or you can have a system which gives you more responsibility, but less stability. The American and the Swiss systems give more stability but less responsibility. The British system on the other hand gives you more responsibility but less stability. The reason for this is obvious. The American executive is a non-parliamentary executive, which means that it is not dependent for its existence upon a majority in the Congress, while the Indian system is a parliamentary executive which means that it is not dependent for its existence upon a majority in the Congress, while the British system is a parliamentary executive which means that it is dependent upon a majority in Parliament. Being a non-parliamentary executive, the Congress of the United States cannot dismiss the executive. A parliamentary government must resign the moment it loses the confidence of a majority of the Members of Parliament. Looking at it from the point of view of responsibility, a non-parliamentary executive being independent of parliament tends to be less responsible to the Legislature, while a parliamentary executive being more dependent upon a majority in Parliament become more responsible. The parliamentary system differs from a non-parliamentary system inasmuch as the former is more responsible than the latter but they also differ as to the time and agency for assessment of their responsibility. Under the non-parliamentary system, such as the one that exists in the U.S.A., the assessment of the responsibility of the executive is periodic. It takes place once in two years. It is done by the electorate. In England, where the parliamentary system prevails, the assessment of responsibility of the executive is both daily and periodic. The daily assessment is done by Members of Parliament, through questions, resolutions, no-confidence motions, adjournment motions and debates on addresses. Periodic assessment is done by the electorate at the time of the election which may take place every five years or earlier. The daily assessment of responsibility which is not available under the American system is felt far more effective than the periodic assessment and far more necessary in a country like India. The Draft Constitution in recommending the parliamentary system of executive has preferred more responsibility to more stability."[22]

Dr. Ambedkar supported parliamentary democracy because Indians were used to this form of government. The British system was a parliamentary democracy. Once the British allowed a greater say for Indians in administration they introduced a similar pattern of governmental operation. Dr. Ambedkar considered this system to be most suitable for the prevailing Indian conditions. The power to legislate was given exclusively to the Parliament.[23]

Thus, Parliament performs a crucial role under the constitutional scheme of India as envisaged by Dr. Ambedkar.

England follows the principle of parliamentary supremacy. As per that principle the Parliament can override all other branches and the scope of interference for other branches is limited. Whereas the situation of Parliament under the Indian Constitution is slightly different. India follows the principle of parliamentary sovereignty subject to the Constitution. Within the contours of the Indian Constitution, the parliament is supreme. The Constitution is supreme and the powers are divided between different organs. All the organs have to operate within their sphere, otherwise the balance would be disturbed. Therefore the Parliament enjoys plenary powers and has to operate within the limitations of the Constitution.[24]

The reason for resting the constituent power with the Parliament was that ultimately it was the Parliament that represented the collective view of the people. It would be disrespect to the views of the people and ultimately democratic principles to let the power of Parliament be subdued by any other branch of institution. The institutional structure ensured that as long as the Parliament did not infract the constitutional guarantees and stayed within the contours of its powers within the Constitution, its exercise is to be respected.

Ambedkar and Powers of President

The position of President under the Indian Constitution is titular, unlike the American President. The President cannot take decisions by himself. President has to act as per the advice of the Council of Ministers. Dr. Ambedkar explained the limitations on the powers of the President in the following words:

"Under the presidential system of America, the President is the chief head of the executive. The administration is vested in him. Under the Draft Constitution the President occupies the same position as the King under the English Constitution. He is the head of the State but not of the executive. He represents the nation but does not rule the nation. He is the symbol of the nation. His place in the administration is that of a ceremonial device on a seal by which the nation's decisions are made known. Under the American Constitution, the President has under him secretaries in charge of different departments. In like manner, the President of the Indian Union will have under him ministers in charge of different departments of administration. Here again there is a fundamental difference between the two. The President of the United States is not bound to accept any advice tendered to him by any of his secretaries. The President of the Indian Union will be generally bound by the advice of his ministers. He can do nothing contrary to their advice nor can he do anything without their advice. The President of the United States can dismiss any secretary at any time. The President of the Indian Union has no power to do so as long as his ministers command a majority in Parliament."[25]

The role of President is limited. The President has the power to give assent to the legislations (known as 'Bills') passed by both the Houses of Parliament. The President can return a Bill for reconsideration but if it is passed again, then the President has to sign it. In the case of budget (known as 'money Bill'), the President has no power to return it. The President has to sign it.[26] Except for signing the Bills and the power to return a Bill for consideration, except a money bill, the President has no control over the power of the Parliament to make and change laws. Most importantly, the President cannot interfere with the power of Parliament to amend the Constitution of India.

In the ordinary course, the Parliament can delegate legislative powers, but it cannot delegate these powers beyond a point. If the delegation is excessive, then that would be unconstitutional.[27] The Parliament has to set out the legislative policy behind a law and cannot delegate this essential power to any other authority.[28]

Although the Indian Parliament is not strictly a supreme body, in practice the Parliament is 'omni-competent' as the British Parliament, subject to restrictions within the Constitution.[29]

Separation of Powers and Jammu & Kashmir

Under the Indian Constitution, the legislative powers of the Union are granted to the Parliament. These powers are exclusive and other authorities cannot take them over. The Parliament can never be bypassed. The legislative power of the Parliament cannot be defeated or taken away. It is the sole repository of legislative actions. Any legislation, including amendment of the Constitution, has to be taken by Parliament.

The executive cannot do things by itself. The executive through the President may exercise legislative powers to the limited extent of issuing ordinance.[30] The ordinance-making power is subject to the control of Parliament. An ordinance has to be taken to the Parliament for ratification. An ordinance would lapse if not passed within six weeks from the time of first assembly of the Parliament or passing of resolutions by the Parliament, disapproving the ordinance.[31] If it fails, then the ordinance cannot be continued. Furthermore, an ordinance cannot be continued without putting it for approval of the Parliament.[32] If ordinances are continued without taking them to the Parliament then that is contrary to the scheme of the Constitution. Except the power of issuance of ordinance subject to strict conditions, there is no permission to the President to legislate. Its competence cannot be taken away by any other body.[33] Any other branch of government or any other body cannot direct the Parliament to make or change laws.[34] If any other branch takes away the power of Parliament to legislate, then it is contrary to parliamentary sovereignty and the Constitution. Except Parliament, no other legislative body, such as state legislature of any state, can claim to be sovereign. Sovereignty rests with the Parliament. Parliament directly represents the people of India. It is based on universal adult suffrage. It is the most representative body in India. No other branch claims that status in the Indian Constitution. Therefore, other branches cannot claim sovereignty that the Parliament exercises. During the drafting of provisions relating to the manner of choice of President, some members in the Constituent Assembly insisted that the President has to be directly elected. The suggestion was rejected by the Constituent Assembly.[35] The reason was that Parliament has to be the sovereign body since it represents the people of India. Only the Parliament is sovereign, not the executive or legislature. It possesses constituent power. Other branches of government do not have these powers.

The discussion above shows that the position of Parliament is central in the Indian Constitution. Within the three branches, the powers are separated. One branch is not allowed to interfere into the affairs of another. All these principles are turned on its head in the case of Jammu & Kashmir. Despite these limitations, the President has become a central figure in the affairs relating to Jammu & Kashmir. The President has taken over the function of Parliament. Most important, the President has taken over the constituent power to amend the Constitution in relation to Jammu & Kashmir. The discussion of separation of powers is pertinent in the context of Jammu & Kashmir.

The power of the President is limited to apply the provisions of the Indian Constitution with "exceptions and modifications". The President is not allowed to amend the provisions of Indian Constitution while applying them to the state of Jammu & Kashmir. Doing so would disturb separation of powers being the executive, i.e. the President would be exercising powers of the legislature, i.e. Parliament. In 1954, the President issued Constitution (Application to Jammu & Kashmir) Order, 1954. Through this order the President added Article 35 A to the Indian Constitution. The President inserted a provision into the Indian Constitution without obtaining the permission of the Parliament, Article 370 (1) (d) allowed the President only to extend the existing provisions of the Constitution with exceptions and modifications. The President was not authorised to amend the Constitution and insert new provisions. Doing so violates the scheme of separation of powers and infraction of powers of Parliament by the executive.

The Supreme Court upheld the power of the President to 'amend' the Constitution of India in *Puranlal Lakhanpal vs The President of India and Others 1961, AIR, 1519.* The court squarely failed to recognise the role of separation of powers in defining the relationship between the three organs of the state. It has been discussed above that separation of powers is a basic feature of the Constitution of India. Since the decision upholding the power of the President to amend the Constitution was prior to the decision of larger bench of the Supreme Court, the earlier decisions have been ignored.

The action of President amending the Constitution and exonerating it from judicial review disturbs the balance of separation of powers envisioned by Dr. Ambedkar. Most importantly, it undermines Parliamentary democracy - a creation of Dr. Ambedkar and allows the President to perform functions that Dr. Ambedkar conceived ought not to be performed.

The Constitution (Application to Jammu & Kashmir) Order, 1954 issued by the President not only amends the Constitution and adds a provision to the Indian Constitution through a backdoor, but also impinges upon the power of the Parliament to amend the Constitution. The order was purportedly applied to extend provisions of the Indian Constitution to Jammu & Kashmir. Under the garb of application of Indian Constitution, the President amended the provisions of the Constitution. The amendment was not effective for the rest of the country, but applied only in the case of Jammu & Kashmir. The shocking part is that the President has made far-reaching changes to the Indian Constitution. There is hardly an important constitutional provision that Dr. Ambedkar introduced in the Constitution that has not been tinkered with.

Article 368

Article 368 is the power of the Parliament to amend the Constitution. It represents the constituent power of the Parliament. Article 368 states:

"368. Power of Parliament to amend the Constitution and procedure therefor.—(1) Notwithstanding anything in this Constitution, Parliament may in exercise of its constituent power amend by way of addition, variation or repeal any provision of this Constitution in accordance with the procedure laid down in this Article.

(2) An amendment of this Constitution may be initiated only by the introduction of a Bill for the purpose in either House of Parliament, and when the Bill is passed in each House by a majority of the total membership of that House and by a majority of not less than two-thirds of the members of that House present and voting, it shall be presented to the President who shall give his assent to the Bill and thereupon the Constitution shall stand amended in accordance with the terms of the Bill:

Provided that if such amendment seeks to make any change in

(a) Article 54, Article 55, Article 73, Article 162 or Article 241, or

(b) Chapter IV of Part V, Chapter V of Part VI, or Chapter I of Part XI, or (c) any of the Lists in the Seventh Schedule, or

(d) the representation of states in Parliament, or

(e) the provisions of this article

The amendment shall also require to be ratified by the legislatures of not less than one-half of the states by resolutions to that effect passed by those legislatures before the Bill-making provision for such amendment is presented to the President for assent.

(3) Nothing in Article 13 shall apply to any amendment made under this Article.

(4) No amendment of this Constitution (including the provisions of Part III) made or purporting to have been made under this Article, whether before or after the commencement of Section 55 of the Constitution (Forty-second Amendment) Act, 1976] shall be called in question in any court on any ground.

(5) For the removal of doubts, it is hereby declared that there shall be no limitation whatever on the constituent power of Parliament to amend by way of addition, variation

or repeal the provisions of this Constitution under this Article."

Through the Presidential Order of 1954, the President also amended Article 368 and added proviso to Article 368 limiting the powers of the Parliament. Article 368 gives the power to the Parliament to amend the Constitution in the following words:

"The Order of 1954 added a proviso curtailing the powers of the Parliament in the following words:

"Provided further that no such amendment shall have effect in relation to the state of Jammu & Kashmir unless applied by order of the President under Clause (1) of Article 370."

The effect of the proviso is that the power given to the Parliament to amend the Constitution has been curtailed by the President through an order. As was discussed above, separation of powers, which is a basic feature of the Constitution, stipulates that one branch cannot interfere in the activities of another. But the situation with regard to Jammu & Kashmir is much serious. Parliament's powers are not only interfered with, but are even curtailed. Curtailment of powers of Parliament is an attack on the foundational value of parliamentary democracy. The power that is curtailed is not an ordinary power; it is the constituent power – a sovereign power. The sovereign power of the Parliament is granted by the Constitution and only the Constitution can take it away. Constitution authorises only the Parliament to amend the Constitution – neither the government nor the courts can do it.

Dr. Ambedkar was clear that there should not be too many restrictions on the power of Parliament to amend the Constitution, like the American Constitution where amendments are virtually impossible. He wanted to retain a certain amount of flexibility.[36] The freedom and flexibility of the Parliament to amend the Constitution has been interfered in the case of Jammu & Kashmir. Again the proviso limiting the powers of the President was not taken to the Parliament, whereas only the Parliament has the power to curtail its powers. The President usurped the functions of the Parliament in relation to Jammu & Kashmir.[37]

The disturbing fact is that the constitutional scheme envisaged by Dr. Ambedkar was trampled to give effect to a political agreement between two leaders Pandit Nehru and Sheikh Abdullah. The Constitution (Application to Jammu & Kashmir), Order, 1954 was issued after the Delhi Accord between Pandit Nehru and Sheikh Abdullah. Dr. Ambedkar wanted the Constitution to remain a neutral document. It was to create an institution that would regulate politics and not institutions that would be disrespected for politics. The Constitution does not allow interference with its fundamental provisions to give effect to political agreements between some influential leaders. Dr. Ambedkar's idea behind creating the structure of the present Constitution was to keep it insulated from the changing whims of the ruling class. If the government was allowed to interfere with the Constitution, then they would make the very structure unworkable. Precisely this warranty was breached by the changes brought about by the President under the 1954 Order.

By making the power of the Parliament to amend the Constitution subject to whims of a state government – not even Central executive – the powers of the Parliament, as conceived by Dr. Ambedkar, were defeated. Taking away of power of Parliament to amend the Constitution is an unreasonable interference with the balance between the three limbs of the government. The tipping of balance not only undermines the institutions but also creates a potential situation for violation of fundamental rights. This situation is seen to have taken place in the case of Jammu & Kashmir, where the fundamental rights have been violated by the executive by amending the Constitution without going to the Parliament and excluding the judiciary from reviewing such an action. These aspects are discussed in detail in the following chapter.

References

1. Constitution of India, Article 79
2. Ibid, Art. 80 for its composition and other details
3. Ibid, Art. 81 for its composition and other details
4. Ibid, Art. 53
5. Above note 1, Chapter IV
6. This is achieved through the writ jurisdiction. Any person can approach the Supreme Court under Article 32 and any High Court under Article 226 challenges a law or the action of the executive on the ground that it violates fundamental rights
7. C.K. Thakker, *Administrative Law*, Eastern Book Company (1992), pp. 30-40
8. Fertiliser Corporation Kamgar Union vs. Union of India, (1981) SCC 568; Narendra Kumar Maheshwari vs. Union of India, 1990 Suppl. SCC 440
9. In re Delhi Laws Act 1912, 1951 SCR 747; Ram Jawaya Kapur vs. State of Punjab, (1955) 2 SCR 225
10. Above note 9 (Ram Jawaya) 225
11. State of Himachal Pradesh vs. Umed Ram Sharma (1986), 2 SCC 68
12. Above note 9 (In re Delhi) SCR 747
13. M P Jain, *Indian Constitutional Law* (6th edn, revised by Samaraditya Pal and Ruma Pal, Vol.2, Lexis Nexis Butterworths Wadhwa, 2010), p. 258
14. L. Chandra Kumar vs. Union of India (1997) 3 SCC 261; Mahmadhusen Abdulrahim Kalota Shaikh (2) vs. Union of India (2009) 2 SCC 1; IR Coelho vs. State of Tamil Nadu (2007) 2 SCC 1
15. Constituent Assembly Debates Official Report (*CAD*) Reprint by Lok Sabha Secretariat, New Delhi (2009), Book 2, Vol. VII, pp. 31-2
16. I.C Golak Nath & Ors vs. State of Punjab & Anr, 1967 (2) SCR 762
17. Indira Nehru Gandhi vs. Shri Raj Narain and Anr., 1975 Supp SCC 1
18. Kesavananda Bharati vs. State of Kerala and Anr. (1973) 4 SCC 225
19. Above note 14 (Coelho)
20. Sir Ivor Jennings, *Constitutional Laws of the Commonwealth,* Vol. I, Oxford: Clarendon Press (1957), p. 49
21. Raja Ram Pal vs. Hon'ble Speaker, Lok Sabha & ors. (2007), 3 SCC 184, para 23
22. Above note 15, p. 32
23. Ibid, pp. 31-37
24. UP Assembly Case (Special Reference No. 1 of 1964) (1965), 1 SCR 413

25. Above note 15, p. 32
26. Above note 1, Art. 111
27. Above note 9 (In re Delhi)
28. Ibid, 747
29. Above note 13, p. 161
30. Above note 1, Art.123
31. Ibid, Art. 123 (2)
32. D.C Wadhwa vs. State of Bihar (1987) 1 SCC (Constitution Bench judgment)
33. Above note 13, p. 161
34. Union of India vs. Prakash P. Hinduja (2003), 6 SCC 195
35. Above note 15, pp. 997-8
36. Ibid, pp. 33
37. By President it does not mean the President *per se*, but the executive – the Prime Minister and the Council of Ministers. Enclosure of Letter by Rajendra Prasad to Jawaharlal Nehru on 6th September, 1952 objecting to this

❐

6

Consequences of Constitution (Application to Jammu & Kashmir) Order, 1954

There are many foundational values introduced in the Constitution of India by Dr. Ambedkar that have been trampled in the case of Jammu & Kashmir. The last chapter discussed the manner in which the Parliament was bypassed and the Constitution was amended. The chapter focused on the unconscionable manner in which the President took over and curtained the powers of the Parliament as envisaged in the Constitution.

The manner in which the constitutional mechanism for the Constitution (Application to Jammu & Kashmir) Order, 1954 issued by the President in violation of the scheme of separation of powers made sweeping interferences with the Constitution of India as conceived by Dr. Ambedkar. The violations are far reaching. They defeat the vision of Dr. Ambedkar and are contrary to be very notions of constitutionalism. In addition to amending the Constitution without going to the Parliament and curtailing amending powers of the Parliament – discussed in the last chapter – the President also reduced other legislative powers of the Parliament stipulated under the Seventh Schedule. The manner in which the powers and prestige of the Parliament is damaged and undermined in relation to legislative subjects and residuary power are discussed in the first section of this chapter.

In the case of Jammu & Kashmir, it is not only the institutions that Dr. Ambedkar created are damaged and undermined, also rights of citizens are trampled. The manner in which fundamental rights are violated is disused in the next chapter. The second section in this chapter attends to the manner in which special rights are created for the residents of Jammu & Kashmir in violation of Dr. Ambedkar's vision of a unified country with single citizenship. The third section discusses the deprivation of rights of Scheduled Tribes in Jammu & Kashmir. Special provisions have been made for \ members of Scheduled Tribes throughout India. The state of Jammu & Kashmir has declined those rights based on the Constitution (Application to Jammu & Kashmir) Order, 1954.

Distribution of Legislative Subjects between Parliament and State Legislature

The Constitution stipulates division of legislative subjects between the Centre and the state. Some legislative subjects are reserved for the Centre, i.e. the Parliament of India, some are reserved for the sate legislature and there is a set of subjects on which both Centre and state have powers to make laws. The Parliament and State legislatures cannot step outside the stipulated subjects. The freedom to legislate earmarked for the legislative body is called legislative competence. Article 245 (1) sets out the territorial jurisdiction of legislations in the following words:

"245. Extent of laws made by Parliament and by the Legislatures of States—(1) Subject to the provisions of this Constitution, Parliament may make laws for the whole or any part of the territory of India, and the Legislature of a State may make laws for the whole or any part of the State."

The powers of the Parliament under Article 245 are plenary and the only limitation on the power to legislate is in the provisions of the Constitution.[1]

The Seventh Schedule of the Constitution sets out the division of subjects which specifies the fields of exercise of legislative powers. This Schedule contains the lists of subjects on which the Parliament and the state legislatures can make laws. There are three lists in the Seventh Schedule: Union List, State List and Concurrent List. The Union List consists of subjects on which the Parliament has exclusive power to make legislations.[2] The State List consists of subject on which the state government has exclusive power to legislate[3] and the Concurrent List contains subjects on which both the Centre and state can legislate.[4] In case of irreconcilable conflict between the laws made by the Centre and the state under their respective entries, the Central laws would prevail.[5] The power of the state legislature to make laws is made subject to the exercise of power by the Parliament to legislate. The structure of the lists was a thoughtful exercise by Dr. Ambedkar.

In other federal countries, such as Australia, the list of subjects in the list for Centre is small. The list of subjects in the concurrent list is long. Dr. Ambedkar did not adopt this; he modified it. The subjects on which the Centre can legislate and the concurrent list where the Centre and state can both legislate was deliberately kept long. Dr. Ambedkar wanted to create a strong Centre. This structure was necessary to keep the country together.[6] This structure of division of legislative competence between the Centre and states, which is applicable uniformly throughout India, has been disturbed in the case of Jammu & Kashmir. This balance was disturbed by the Constitution (Application to Jammu & Kashmir) Order, 1954.

The subjects mentioned in the Seventh Schedule cannot comprehensively cover all the subjects on which laws are required to be made. There are many matters outside the purview of the lists. The power to legislate on such matters is called 'residual power'. The 'residual power' is exclusively with the Parliament.[7] In order to create a strong Centre, it was necessary that residual powers are given to the Parliament and the Parliament also enjoys the power to supersede the state legislatures on certain issues. Residual power includes vital powers, such as power to impose taxes on matters not mentioned in any of the lists.[8] The residual power that belongs to the Parliament and so granted thoughtfully by Dr. Ambedkar to Parliament has been transferred to Jammu & Kashmir by the Constitution (Application to Jammu & Kashmir) Order, 1954. This is achieved by excluding the exclusive power of Parliament to legislate on residual subjects. The plenary residual power of the Parliament has been limited only to certain stipulated situations. The Constitution (Application to Jammu & Kashmir) Order 1954 restricts the residual power of the Parliament only to those subjects mentioned in the Order. The subjects covered under this order are:

a) terrorist activities aimed at overawing the government as by law established or striking terror in the people or any section of the people or alienating any section of the people or adversely affecting the harmony amongst different sections of the people;
b) other activities aimed at directed questioning or disrupting the sovereignty and territorial integrity of India or bringing about cession of a part of the territory of India or secession of a part of the territory of India from the Union or causing insult to the Indian National Flag, the Indian National Anthem and the Constitution;
c) taxes on foreign travel by air or sea, inland travel by air, postal articles, including money orders, phonograms and telegrams.

Power to impose taxes on residual subjects has been retained by the state government. Except these limited topics the Parliament cannot legislate on any other subject not covered under the Seventh Schedule.

In national interest, if the Rajya Sabha authorises by a resolution, the Parliament can pass a law on a subject in the State List.[9] This power of the Parliament is inapplicable in Jammu & Kashmir[10] although Rajya Sabha and Lok Sabha have representatives elected from Jammu & Kashmir. All these provisions of the Constitution were adopted by the Constituent Assembly without much debate. There was an agreement with the framework that Dr. Ambedkar had in mind while these provisions were drafted. Interestingly, all these provisions existed in the Constitution but were made inapplicable to Jammu & Kashmir by the Constitution (Application to Jammu & Kashmir) Order, 1954.

The provisions introduced in the Constitution of India through the Constitution (Application to Jammu & Kashmir) Order, 1954 are unconstitutional. They contradict the Constitution of India as well as the Constitution of Jammu & Kashmir. The Constitution of Jammu & Kashmir has fully recognised the powers of the Parliament without any limitations. Section 5 of the Constitution of Jammu & Kashmir is very clear when it says:

"Section 5: Extent of executive and legislative power of the state: The executive and legislative power of the State extends to all matters except those with respect to which Parliament has power to make laws for the State under the provisions of the Constitution of India."

As per the standard rule of interpretation *lex posterior derogat lega priori* subsequent provision supersedes older provision. Section 5 of the Constitution of Jammu & Kashmir came into force on 26 January 1957 and the Constitution (Application to Jammu & Kashmir) Order, 1954 was issued on 14 May 1954. The Constitution of Jammu & Kashmir having come into force later would supersede the Constitution (Application to Jammu & Kashmir) Order, 1954 on the point of scope of legislative powers of the Parliament. The experience is that despite this effect, the state of Jammu & Kashmir continues to claim disproportionate and unconstitutional share of legislative power in comparison to the Parliament.

The structures conceptualised and strong legislative interlink between Centre and state introduced by Dr. Ambedkar have been discarded in its application to Jammu & Kashmir. The so-called justification to do so is Article 370. As was alluded to in prior chapters, Article 370 was only a temporary provision. The Constituent Assembly, including Dr. Ambedkar was persuaded to support the provision with the express understanding that provision was to last only until the time the Constituent Assembly of Jammu & Kashmir is constituted and it performs its function of Constitution-making. In spite of this clear understanding, even after the Constituent Assembly of Jammu & Kashmir finished its functions in 17 November 1956, Article 370 has continued. The most disturbing fact is that it is now being claimed to be a permanent feature or a provision which was said by the Constitution-makers of India as temporary but has somehow magically become special.[11]

Special Rights of Residents of Jammu & Kashmir

One of the features of federation is dual polity. Dual polity implies separate structures in the Centre and in states and consequentially dual citizenship. In a conventional federal structure such as U.S.A, a person has two citizenships: of the Centre as well as the states. Dr. Ambedkar did not want such a situation to exist in India. He was resolute that there should be only a single citizenship applicable to all Indians uniformly. Stating that India is a country with single citizenship, Dr. Ambedkar stated in the Constituent Assembly:

"The proposed Indian Constitution is a dual polity with a single citizenship. There is only one citizenship for the whole of India. It is Indian citizenship. There is no state citizenship.

Every Indian has the same rights of citizenship, no matter in what state he resides."[12]

India's constitutional structure defining the relationship between the Union and states is different from the federal structure as understood conventionally. In countries, such as the U.S.A. it is very different. There are a wide range of regulations that may be imposed by the governments at the state level because the residents of those states are treated as citizens of that state. Describing the peculiarity of a federal structure and distinguishing it from the Indian constitutional scheme Dr. Ambedkar said:

"Each state has also certain rights in its own domain that it holds for the special advantage of its own citizens. Thus wild game and fish in a sense belong to the state. It is customary for the states to charge higher hunting and fishing licence fees to non-residents than to its own citizens. The states also charge non-residents higher tuition in state colleges and universities, and permit only residents to be admitted to their hospitals and asylums except in emergencies.

"In short, there are a number of rights that a state can grant to its own citizens or residents that it may and does legally deny to non-residents, or grant to non-residents only on more difficult terms than those imposed on residents. These advantages, given to the citizen in his own state, constitute the special rights of state citizenship. Taken all together, they amount to a considerable difference in rights between citizens and non-citizens of the state. The transient and the temporary sojourner is everywhere under some special handicaps.

"The proposed Indian Constitution is a dual polity with a single citizenship. There is only one citizenship for the whole of India. It is Indian citizenship. There is no state citizenship. Every Indian has the same rights of citizenship, no matter in what state he resides."[13]

Dual citizenship gives certain special rights and privileges to citizens of the state. Citizens of the country who are not citizens of the state are excluded from enjoying those rights and privileges. In addition to being discriminatory, such a system creates immense practical difficulties for people. The problems faced in the US are illuminating. Since in US there is citizenship of the state as well as the Federation (or Centre/ Union), the states can impose restrictions on political rights within the state. The political rights that could be restricted include the right to vote and holding of public office. States may discriminate in favour of their own citizens. This favouritism for state citizens could extend to other matters as well, such as obtaining employment in the service of the state or local government. In these cases, a person would have to be a citizen of that state to get a job with the government. The citizenship-based restrictions are extended to practicing other professions, such as law and medicine, etc. Dr. Ambedkar explained these problems in the Constituent Assembly in the following words:

"Each state has also certain rights in its own domain that it holds for the special advantage of its own citizens. Thus wild game and fish in a sense belong to the state. It is customary for the States to charge higher hunting and fishing licence fees to non-residents than to its own citizens. The states also charge non-residents higher tuition in state colleges and universities, and permit only residents to be admitted to their hospitals and asylums except in emergencies.

"In short, there are a number of rights that a state can grant to its own citizens or residents that it may and does legally deny to non-residents, or grant to non-residents only on more difficult terms than those imposed on residents. These advantages, given to the citizen in his own state, constitute the special rights of state citizenship. Taken all together, they amount to a considerable difference in rights between citizens and non-citizens of the state. The transient and the temporary sojourner is everywhere under some special handicaps."

Any such discrimination is disallowed in the Indian Constitution because we do not follow dual citizenship in India.

India does not have citizenship of each state. There is only one citizenship and that is of India. By virtue of having single citizenship, the rights of all Indian citizens are same and all citizens are equal throughout the country. They are not dependent on the place where she resides. The state of residence is irrelevant. The only permissible ground for discrimination is of domicile. The restrictions that could be imposed under the rules of domicile are limited. The rules cannot violate fundamental rights of citizens. The limitation could be in the form of need of residence in the state for a certain number of years. Restrictions cannot be based merely on place of birth. There has to be flexibility in acquiring domicile. A state cannot, under the garb of imposing conditions of domicile, deprive people permanently from the possibility of obtaining domicile. The rationale for the restrictions is that considering that it should not happen that someone merely passing by the state takes over employment and excludes those who have been residing in the state for a very long time. Since the residents of a state who are domiciled, contribute revenue to the state. If residents of other states are taking a share from that revenue through government employment, then they should first contribute by staying in the state for some time and acquire domicile. The rules on domicile contemplate few and limited restrictions being imposed on citizens by state governments. The states could impose some restrictions but not beyond the requirements of domicile. He clearly exposed the underlying philosophy:

"It is the feeling of many persons in this House that, since we have established a common citizenship throughout India, irrespective of the local jurisdiction of the provinces and the Indian states, it is only a concomitant thing that residents should not be required for holding a particular post in a particular state because, insofar as you make residence a qualification, you are really subtracting from the value of a common citizenship which we have established by this Constitution or which we propose to establish by this Constitution. Therefore, in my judgement, the argument that residence should not be a qualification to hold appointments under the state is a perfectly valid and a perfectly sound argument. At the same time, it must be realised that you cannot allow people who are flying from one province to another, from one state to another, as mere birds of passage without any roots, without any connection with that particular province, just to come, apply for posts and, so to say, take the plums and walk away. Therefore, some limitation is necessary. It was found, when this matter was investigated, that already today in very many provinces, rules have been framed by the provincial governments prescribing a certain period of residence as a qualification for a post in that particular province. Therefore, the proposal in the amendment that, although as a general rule residence should not be a qualification, yet some exception might be made, is not quite out of the ordinary. We are merely following the practice which has been already established in the various provinces. However, what we found was that while different provinces were laying down a certain period as a qualifying period for posts, the periods varied considerably. Some provinces said that a person must be actually domiciled. What that means, one does not know. Others have fixed ten years, some seven years and so on. It was therefore felt that, while it might be desirable to fix a period as a qualifying test, that qualifying test should be uniform throughout India. Consequently, if that object is to be achieved, viz. that the qualifying residential period should be uniform, that object can be achieved only by giving the power to Parliament and not giving it to the local units, whether provinces or states. That is the underlying purpose of this amendment putting down residence as a qualification."[14]

Except for the limited provisions under domicile no further restrictions can be imposed on Indian citizens. Their rights throughout the country are uniform and unalterable.

Dr. Ambedkar never conceived that under the Indian Constitution a citizen of India residing in one state would be deprived of the right to vote, hold political office, practice profession and claim employment with the government in another state merely for the reason that the person was not born in the state. Dr. Ambedkar abhorred such a practice. The treatment of citizens had to be equal throughout India. The conditions for obtaining domicile are to be uniform throughout India. There cannot be any restrictions except the period of stay required. Conditions of domicile cannot be based on the place of birth. Article 15 (1) does not allow discrimination on the place of birth.

"15. Prohibition of discrimination on grounds of religion, race, caste, sex or place of birth—(1) The State shall not discriminate against any citizen on grounds only of religion, race, caste, sex, place of birth or any of them."

The position in Jammu & Kashmir is contrary to this constitutional objective of Dr. Ambedkar. In Jammu & Kashmir residents of other states are not allowed a government job, nor allowed to vote in state and local elections or hold public office in the state. The restriction applies even to those who have always resided and continue to reside in Jammu & Kashmir but are not 'permanent residents'. In Jammu & Kashmir, citizen-like rights are created in favour of a special category called 'permanent residents'. Permanent residents are defined in Section 6 of the Jammu & Kashmir Constitution.

Special rights and privileges are awarded to permanent residents and fundamental rights of others are violated. The domicile requirement is based on stay for a certain duration. In Jammu & Kashmir, the rule has been applied in such a manner that nobody can become a permanent resident. The residents of the state are called permanent residents. The manner of determination of a permanent resident is provided in Section 6 of the Jammu & Kashmir Constitution. In addition to being a citizen of India, one could become a permanent resident on following conditions:

a) State subject of Class I and II under the rule of Maharaja; and
b) Settled in Jammu & Kashmir prior to 14 May 1944.

a) *State subject*

The erstwhile rulers introduced the concept of state subject. Through the notifications of 20 April 1927 and 27 June 1932, five categories of persons were declared as state subjects.

First, all persons born and residing in the state before the commencement of the reign of Maharaja Gulab Singh and persons who settled in the region before the commencement of *Samvat* year 1942 and continued to reside permanently in the state thereafter. These were called Class I state subjects

Second, all persons except Class I, who were residing within the state before the close of the *Samvat* year 1968 and thereafter resided permanently in the state and acquired immovable property. These were called Class II state subjects.

Third, all persons other than Class I and II, permanently residing within the state and acquired immovable property under a *rayatnama* or under *ijazatnama* and could execute *rayatnama* after ten years of continuous residence in the state. These persons were called Class III state subjects.

Fourth, companies that were registered in the state and in which the government was financially interested or the government was satisfied that they gave some economic benefit or financial stability to the state and were declared state subjects by special order of the ruler.

Fifth, foreign nationals could acquire state subject after attaining 18 years of age and purchasing property under *ijazatnama* or obtaining a *rayatnama* after 10 years of continuous residence in the state.

The definition of state subject was open and allowed companies and other persons not originally from or born in the state of Jammu & Kashmir to obtain state subject. The permanent resident definition under Section 6 destroyed this flexibility. It allowed only persons from the first two categories, i.e. Class I and II to become permanent residents. The rest, although being state subjects, were declined permanent resident status. Therefore companies that were allowed to conduct business in Jammu & Kashmir, persons that had obtained an *ijazatnama* or *rayatnama* and foreigners who were allowed to settle were excluded from becoming permanent residents. In addition to being discriminatory against those who do not belong to the state of Jammu & Kashmir, Section 6 is discriminatory even between those who belong to the state. This was a form of discrimination abhorred by Dr. Ambedkar and would be discussed under the topic of fundamental rights in the next chapter.

Further the state subjects of the first two categories: Class I and II who migrated to Pakistan after 1 March 1947 and returned before 14 May 1954 under a permit for resettlement in the state for permanent return issued by or under the authority of any law made by the state legislature are treated as permanent residents. Others who resided in the state as state subjects, except Class I and II are not treated as state subjects even if they have lived in the state all their life.

The power of determining citizenship is exclusively with the Centre. This is necessary for protecting the security and integrity of India. In the case of Jammu & Kashmir, this provision has been tinkered with. At the time of Partition, after having moved to Pakistan or Bangladesh, if a permanent resident suddenly decides to return to Jammu & Kashmir, she can do so without the need of any authorisation from the Central Government. The state government can grant a permit of resettlement for such a person. In view of the well-known involvement of Pakistan in terrorist activities in the state, the state government is not well equipped to decide whether a person who is granted resettlement permit should be allowed to settle in any Indian territory or not. Details of information and security are only with the agencies of the Central Government.

This provision again interferes with the power of the Central Government on its exclusive domain for grant of citizenship. Dr. Ambedkar had made it very clear that the power of deciding questions of citizenship would remain exclusively with the Centre. The states do not have any power in this regard.

b) *Settled prior to 14 May 1944*

The Constitution of Jammu & Kashmir was adopted on 17 November 1956 and came into force on 26 January 1957. The state Constituent Assembly retrospectively declared that if a person is not a state subject, then the person who has lawfully acquired property or ordinarily resided in the state 10 years prior would become a permanent resident. Thus, in effect, only those persons who have settled in the state of Jammu & Kashmir by lawfully acquiring property or were ordinary residents prior to 14 May 1944 would be entitled to become permanent residents. The choice of date of 14 May 1944 is arbitrary. It ensure that those who entered the state of Jammu & Kashmir after 1947 are excluded from becoming permanent residents. These conditions show that no one can become a permanent resident except on the basis of birth. There are large groups of persons who are excluded from obtaining permanent resident status. In consequence their fundamental rights have been violated. These and other related issues are discussed in detail in the next chapter.

In addition to creation of a separate category of permanent residents – akin to citizenship, the right to declare who should become permanent resident is reserved by the

State Legislature under Section 8 of the Jammu & Kashmir Constitution. Section 8 says:

Nothing in the foregoing provisions of this part shall derogate from the power of the State Legislature to make any law defining the classes of persons who are, or shall be, permanent residents of the State."

Furthermore, the Constitution of Jammu & Kashmir gives the liberty to the state of Jammu & Kashmir to grant special privileges to permanent residents.[15] All the rights under the Constitution of India, including fundamental rights, are reserved exclusively for permanent residents.[16] Others are excluded from these rights. Thus the state government cannot take away life and liberty of a permanent resident, but it can of any person who is a citizen of India but not a permanent resident. As would be discussed in the next chapter, this is affront to the very notion of fundamental rights introduced by Dr. Ambedkar to protect citizens from excesses of governments.

In this view, there is a deeper thought that reflects Dr. Ambedkar's statesmanship. He could see that there was a scope for regionalism to foster in India. If it did, then a state could raise barriers to discriminate between residents of the state and people residing in other states of India. The Constitution created single citizenship. A person cannot be discriminated while moving in any other state. Any such effort would defeat the objective of creating a unified India. His very vision has been defeated in the case of Jammu & Kashmir. The state has asserted more powers that the federal Constitution of India would allow, as desired by Dr. Ambedkar. The present situation of Jammu & Kashmir where the state is claiming greater power defeats Indian federalism and Dr. Ambedkar's ideals.

Protection of Scheduled Tribes

The situation of Scheduled Tribes was a pressing issue for

the Constituent Assembly. People of these communities had taken an active part in the freedom struggle. They had remained in their regions but continued to fight for Independence. In the era of a modern and independent India, it was necessary to engage them in the mainstream while ensuring that their ways of life are conserved and respected. A balance had to be maintained. It was important that adequate protective mechanisms are put in place. Alongside, appropriate ways had to be made for persons belonging to these communities to get modern education so that they grow to their fullest potential and participate in the political process of the country. Dr. Ambedkar always stood for the downtrodden and marginalised groups. It was only natural for him to support the cause of Scheduled Tribes and make provision for their amelioration through provisions in the Constitution of India.

The term 'Scheduled Tribes' was coined by Dr. Ambedkar for the convenience of identifying them. Until then, they were referred as '*Adibasis*' in the Constituent Assembly debates.

Dr. Ambedkar was conscious of the logistical difficulty in identifying tribal people. The first task was of earmarking them. Two categories of areas were identified: scheduled areas and scheduled tribal areas. The tribal areas relate to the present state of Assam. There are tribals in other parts of the country as well. To earmark them, these areas are called scheduled areas.[17] Dr Ambedkar explained the reason for calling them Scheduled Tribes rather than using the general word *Adibasis*, in the following words:

"Now, coming to the question of the Scheduled Tribes and as to why I substituted the word 'Scheduled' for the word 'aboriginal', the explanation is this. As I said, the word 'Scheduled Tribe' has a fixed meaning, because it enumerates the tribes, as you will see in the two Schedules. Well, the word '*Adibasi*' is really a general term which has no specific legal de jure connotation, something like the untouchables. It is a general term; anybody may include anybody in the term `untouchable'. It has no definite legal connotation. That is why in the Government of India Act of 1935, it was felt necessary to give the word `untouchable' some legal connotation and the only way it was found feasible to do it was to enumerate the communities which in different parts and in different areas were regarded by the local people as satisfying the test of untouchability. The same question may arise with regard to *Adibasis*. Who are the *Adibasis*? And the question will be relevant, because by this Constitution, we are conferring certain privileges, certain rights on these *Adibasis*. In order that, if the matter was taken to a court of law there should be a precise definition as to who are these *Adibasis*, it was decided to invent, so to say, another category or another term to be called 'Scheduled Tribes' and to enumerate the *Adibasis* under that head."[18]

Dr. Ambedkar was aware that the list of Scheduled Tribes is carefully drafted so that important communities are not left out. If he had used the generic word *Adibasis*, it would not have been possible to identify these communities clearly. He therefore used a legal term, Scheduled Tribes. This makes it possible to identify them and give them rights and ways to realise those rights. He kept the list open and allowed local governments to add to the list as and when they realise that some communities have been left out.[19]

To protect the enclosures of residence of Scheduled Tribes, it was thought appropriate to impose restrictions on the right of free movement and the right to settle in any territory of India.[20] The Constitution makes provision for the protection and promotion of Scheduled Tribes in the Constitution. Through the Directive Principles of State Policy, the Constitution-makers in Article 46 tender an advice to the government. The government "shall promote with special case the educational and economic interests of the weaker sections of the people, and, in particular, of the Scheduled Castes and Scheduled Tribes."[21] Article 15 (4) allows a government to make special provision for Scheduled Tribes. In Jammu & Kashmir the special provisions made for Scheduled Tribes are inapplicable. The Constitution (Application to Jammu & Kashmir) Order, 1954 excluded the operation of special provisions for Scheduled Tribes. None of the affirmative action provisions meant for persons from Scheduled Castes are provided for members of Scheduled Tribes residing in Jammu & Kashmir.

Considering the marginalisation of Scheduled Tribes seats have been reserved in Lok Sabha.[22] The number of seats reserved is based on the population.[23] The Constitution also directs that seats be reserved for members of Scheduled Tribes in the State Legislature.[24] The number of seats reserved depends on the population.[25] Reservation of seats for Scheduled Tribes is done in all the State Legislatures in the country, except Jammu & Kashmir. The claims of members of Scheduled Tribes are to be given a due consideration for appointment in services and posts under the Central and the state government.[26] Accordingly seats are reserved for members from tribal communities, but there is no provision in Jammu & Kashmir state for their appointment. The operation of all these provisions for the protection and progress of Scheduled Tribes was excluded by the Constitution (Application to Jammu & Kashmir) Order, 1954.[27]

According to the Special Census conducted by the Registrar General of India, in 1987, out of the total population of 77.19 lakhs of the state of Jammu & Kashmir, Scheduled Casts are 6.41 lakhs, constituting about 8.3 per cent and Scheduled Tribes are about 7.90 lakhs constituting 11 per cent of the total population of the state.[28] In the year 2011, the population of Scheduled Tribes grew to 10. 46 lakhs. The population of Scheduled Tribes is sizeable and larger than Scheduled Castes. There are regions like Kargil and Leh where the population of Scheduled Tribes is 100 per cent and 93 per cent respectively.[29] Although the Constitution provided for affirmative actions for the betterment of Scheduled Tribes since the coming into force of the Jammu & Kashmir Constitution the provision was not applied in Jammu & Kashmir. The state government resisted the application of these provisions. In 1989 the President of India issued the Constitution (Jammu & Kashmir) Scheduled Tribes Order, 1989 and a list of Scheduled Tribes was drawn. It was much later that reservation in government services was given.

The democratic institution established in the state of Jammu & Kashmir after Independence of the country has resisted application of affirmative action that Dr. Ambedkar introduced in the Constitution the India. It is inconceivable to defend non-application of beneficial provisions. People from Scheduled Tribes living in other parts of India availed the protection that Dr. Ambedkar granted them, but residents of Jammu & Kashmir were deprived of those rights for a very long time.

References

1. Indira Gandhi Nehru vs. Raj Narain, 1975 Supplementary SCC 1
2. Constitution of India, Article 246 (1)
3. Ibid, 246 (3)
4. Ibid, 246 (2)
5. State of West Bengal vs. Committee for Protection of Democratic Rights (2010), 3 SCC 571
6. Constituent Assembly Debates Official Report (*CAD*) Reprint by Lok Sabha Secretariat, New Delhi (2009), Book 2, p. 35
7. Constitution of India, Article 248 (1)
8. Ibid, 248 (2)
9. Ibid, 249
10. Article 2 (6), The Constitution (Application to Jammu & Kashmir) Order, 1954
11. A.G. Noorani, *Article 370: A Constitutional History of Jammu & Kashmir*, OUP (2011); A.S. Anand, *The Constitution of Jammu & Kashmir: Its Developments and Comments*, Universal Law Publishing Co. Ltd (2004); State Autonomy Committee Report, General Administration Department, Jammu & Kashmir Government, Srinagar (2000)

12. Above note 6, pp. 34
13. Ibid
14. Ibid, p. 700-1.
15. Section 9, Constitution of Jammu & Kashmir
16. Ibid, Section 10
17. Above note 6, p. 782
18. Ibid, p. 782
19. Ibid, pp. 782-3
20. Above note 2, Article 19 (5)
21. Ibid, Article 46
22. Ibid, 330 (1)
23. Ibid, 330 (2)
24. Ibid, 332 (1)
25. Ibid, 332 (3)
26. Ibid, 335
27. Above note 10, Section 2 (11)
28. Available at ncsc.nic.in/files/ncsc/vol2/96.pdf, p. 52
29. Ibid

❐

7

Fundamental Rights and Jammu & Kashmir

Fundamental rights are the distinguishing factor of the Indian Constitution. The fundamental rights have their deep roots in the struggle for Independence and "they were included in the Constitution in the hope and expectation that one day the tree of true liberty will bloom in India."[1] Fundamental rights have resulted in creation of rich jurisprudence on protection of rights of people in India. This jurisprudence is revered and followed in other jurisdictions as well. The Constituent Assembly was conscious about the important role that fundamental rights were to perform in the democratic society of future India. The entire Constituent Assembly was conscious about the importance of fundamental rights and the need to carefully draft them. A separate committee with further sub-committees was constituted to work on fundamental rights. The Advisory Committee was under the chairmanship of Sardar Vallabhbhai Patel and Acharya Kriplani headed the Fundamental Rights Sub-Committee. The committee discussed the rights that need to be specified in great detail and presented a report to Constituent Assembly.[2]

Dr. Ambedkar was particularly sensitive about protection and upholding of fundamental rights. He incorporated that vision in Part III of the Constitution, which is known as the fundamental rights chapter. He was aware that people were the central entity in the constitutional scheme. The Constitution aimed at creating institutions that would serve people in the best possible fashion. If people were forgotten in the scheme of the Constitution, then the laudable institutions would become hollow structures. While the institutions perform their functions within the contours set out by the Constitution, they have to be careful that they do not interfere with the fundamental rights of people. All citizens of India, irrespective of their place of residence, are entitled for fundamental rights. In some situations even non-citizens enjoy these rights.[3]

Fundamental rights are the very soul of the Constitution that Dr. Ambedkar envisioned. This chapter explores in detail, whether fundamental rights have been respected in Jammu & Kashmir or not? Dr. Ambedkar's vision about fundamental rights achieved in Jammu & Kashmir? This chapter brings to fore the plight of those residents of the state of Jammu & Kashmir, who have lived in the state for almost four generations but are deprived of protection of fundamental rights in the state.

Position of Fundamental Rights in the Constitution of India

Fundamental rights are an important characteristic of the Indian Constitution. There are three categories of rights in the Indian polity: legal rights, constitution rights and fundamental rights. The value and sanctity of the rights is in the ascending order. Legal rights are normally provided in law. The laws are a creature of the legislature and amenable to change. Therefore, legal rights are amenable to the vicissitudes of the legislature. The legislature can remove them as and when it wants to, just as it can grant them. Constitutional rights are rights prescribed in the Constitution. These rights carry a higher value as compared to legal rights because they are derived from the Constitution. However, these rights too are at the mercy of the

Parliament since the Parliament can amend the Constitution and remove or alter these rights. The third category of rights is fundamental rights. Fundamental rights are mentioned in Part III of the Constitution. Their nature is such that they cannot be readily amended. They are a part of the basic structure of the Constitution. Thus the power of Parliament to tinker with them is limited.

Fundamental rights, as the name suggests are rights that are necessary for individuals in a democratic society. They are inalienable and encompass a multitude of rights such as social, economic, political, etc. The rights included within the umbrella of fundamental rights promise protection of life and assure a life with dignity. In the early phases of the Indian Constitution, the Supreme Court considered these rights to be of negative nature: the rights were meant to operate as restrictions on the powers of the government. But soon the Supreme Court became active and started giving positive interpretation to fundamental rights. The Supreme Court has interpreted fundamental rights liberally thereafter.[4] Over the years, the Supreme Court has added various comports to the concept of fundamental rights such as equality, good environment, health and sanitation, basic education and other aspects of human existence necessary for achieving their fuller realisation.[5]

Fundamental rights make the government accountable towards people and put individuals at the centre of the constitutional scheme.[6] The strength of fundamental rights is that any action taken by the government that deprives people of fundamental rights is void. Such actions cannot be sustained.[7] Although fundamental rights are contained in the Constitution, they are not a gift by the government to its citizens. These rights are inherent to all human being by virtue of being humans. In that sense the Constitution does not grant or confer fundamental rights; it simply recognises them. Supreme Court has called these rights as axiomatic.[8] Since the government does not give these rights; the government cannot take them away. No restrictions can be imposed on them except to the extent stipulated in the Constitution. Beyond the limitations mentioned in the Constitution the government cannot add any other limitations on fundamental rights.

Fundamental rights are contained in Part III of the Constitution of India. Part III consists of Articles 12 to 35 which contain different fundamental rights, such as right to life, freedom to settle in any part of the country or practice any profession or occupation or trade, right to equality, equal opportunity in public employment and no discrimination based on sex, religion or place of birth. There are various other rights, including the right to approach the Supreme Court for protection of fundamental rights.

Fundamental rights are enforceable against all branches of government, including judiciary which is responsible for protection of these rights. Dr. Ambedkar could have compromised on non-adherence to any other part of the Constitution, but certainly not with fundamental rights. He was instrumental in emphasising the importance of these rights for a secure future of Indian polity in the Constituent Assembly.

Ambedkar and Fundamental Rights

Dr. Ambedkar had special interest in fundamental rights, which were close to his heart considering his background. Being a Dalit, he was subjected to innumerable instances of mistreatment. These incidents occurred despite his education and enviable prestige that he earned in the world through his scholarship. He understood the value of an egalitarian society for facilitating development of citizens to their fullest potential. He saw the entire set of fundamental rights recognised under Part III of the Constitution as a composite whole. Despite his experience of discrimination based on birth, he was not insistent on protection of only one kind of rights. He supported the entire array of fundamental rights recognised under the

Constitution. Therefore, his views are equally applicable to all kinds of fundamental rights recognised under the Constitution.

The pressing need of the Indian society was removal of inequality and discrimination of all forms. Fundamental rights were to achieve this target Through Article 17, all forms of untouchability were removed. An important step for an equal society is removal of discriminations of all kinds. Article 18 of the Constitution removed titles, which would allow one individual a higher status than others. The accentuating feature of the Constitution is the promise of equality. Article 14 states:

"The State shall not deny to any person equality before the law or the equal protection of the laws within the territory of India."

The promise of equality in Article 14 is a general provision applicable across all aspects of life. In addition to the general directive to governments, specific grounds are also given, based on which, discrimination cannot be done. Article 15 provides:

"Article 15 (1): The State shall not discriminate against any citizen on grounds only of religion, race, caste, sex, place of birth or any of them."

Dr. Ambedkar was an eminent jurist. He had command over jurisprudence of rights and the need to balance the power of state and protect the rights of citizens. It was natural for him to stand in favour of upholding and protecting fundamental rights. Closeness of fundamental rights to Dr. Ambedkar's heart and his expertise on the subject are evident in the speeches delivered by him on various occasions before the Constituent Assembly.

Respect for fundamental rights, according to Dr. Ambedkar, was not an artificial exercise. For him – and rightly so – fundamental rights have "become part and parcel of our mental makeup". When he referred to 'our mental makeup' he was referring to not only international practice but also changing attitude within the Indian society. The modern understanding of human rights emanates from the American and the French revolution. The French Constituent Assembly adopted the Rights of Man. In addition to animating the 'mental makeup' of the Western world, fundamental rights had become influential in Indian society as well. Highlighting their impact on the minds of Indians, despite existing orthodoxy in the Indian society, Ambedkar said:

> "I say they have become not only the part and parcel of the mental makeup of modern man in every civilised part of the world, but also in our own country which is so orthodox, so archaic in its thought and its social structure, hardly anyone can be found to deny its validity."[9]

Like Dr. Ambedkar, for all the Constitution-makers, fundamental rights were so dear to their hearts that they all unanimously supported them. Other members of the Constituent Assembly shared Dr. Ambedkar's vision of fundamental rights as well. Accentuating the role of fundamental rights, N. V. Gadgil said,

"...fundamental rights are, what are most cherished by the common man. They provides freedom of association, freedom of speech and all other civil liberties which are to be (sic) found in the Constitution of every country."[10]

Considering the time constraints, all members of the Constituent Assembly could not speak on fundamental rights. They all had tacit agreement over the need and importance of these rights.

Dr. Ambedkar ensured that they are available against a wide range of authorities, including state governments and territories that formerly formed part of princely states. This is important since the record of human rights in these areas was not very impressive. Moreover the rights were universal and absolute. He was strongly opposed to alteration of fundamental rights by the executive. They are available throughout India and citizens residing in any part can claim them and the content of the right that they can claim remains uniform. No government can claim exception from enforcing these rights. Within the sphere of limitations, they are absolute. In a situation where he eschewed alterations by the Central Government of fundamental rights, there was no question of a state government altering and interfering with the fundamental rights

The proliferation of fundamental rights internationally and in India was natural. Importance of fundamental rights was increasing considering the objectives fundamental rights were to achieve. According to Dr. Ambedkar, fundamental rights have two aspects; first, every citizen possesses these rights and second they are binding upon every authority.[11]

Except for the limitations contained in fundamental rights in the Constitution, fundamental rights cannot be abridged. From fairly early on, in the Constituent Assembly Dr. Ambedkar expressed his insistence on the non-diminishable characteristic of fundamental rights. In the early stages of discussions in the Constituent Assembly, Pandit Nehru presented the Resolution on Aims and Objectives. This Resolution was to form the basis of drafting the future Constitution. Dr. Ambedkar was critical of the Resolution because it provided fundamental rights but never provided remedies for enforcing fundamental rights. Moreover, the fundamental rights were made subject to law and morality. Dr. Ambedkar took a strong exception to subjecting fundamental rights to morality and law. In legal philosophy, scholars have attempted to define morality in a certain identifiable way, but their determinations are inconclusive. In such a situation Dr. Ambedkar's opposition to the introduction of an exception to fundamental rights through a flexible concept of morality was justified.

According to him, if the right to make exceptions to fundamental rights was allowed on the grounds of morality and law, fundamental rights would be at the mercy of the future executive, i.e. the government. The views towards fundamental rights would depend on the government of the day and the executive will keep changing the scope of fundamental rights, depending on its preferences and choices. These activities will make fundamental rights weak and ineffective. It was necessary to insulate fundamental rights from the control of the government. His words were:

"I should have expected him to go much further than he has done in that part of the Resolution. As a student of history, I should have preferred this part of the Resolution not being embodied in it at all. When one reads that part of the Resolution, it reminds one of the Declaration of the Rights of Man which was pronounced by the French Constituent Assembly. I think I am right in suggesting that, after the lapse of practically 450 years, the Declaration of the Rights of Man and the principles which are embodied in it has become part and parcel of our mental makeup. I say they have become not only a part and parcel of the mental make-up of modern man in every civilised part of the world, but also in our own country which is so orthodox, so archaic in its thought and its social structure, hardly anyone can be found to deny its validity To repeat it now as the Resolution does is, to say the least, pure pedantry. These principles have become the silent immaculate premise of our outlook. It is therefore unnecessary to proclaim as forming a part of our creed. The Resolution suffers from certain other lacuna. I find that this part of the Resolution, although it enunciates certain rights, does not speak of remedies. All of us are aware of the fact that rights are nothing unless remedies are provided, whereby people can seek to obtain redress when rights are invaded. I find a complete absence of remedies. Even the usual formula, that no man's life, liberty and property shall be taken without the due process of law, finds no place in the Resolution. These fundamental set out are made subject to law and moralist. Obviously what is law, what is morality will be determined by the Executive of the day and when the Executive may take, one view another Executive may take another view and we do not know what exactly would be the position with regard to fundamental rights, if this matter is left to the Executive of the day. Sir, there are here certain provisions which speak of justice, economical, social and political. If this Resolution has a reality behind it and a sincerity, of which I have not the least doubt, coming as it does from the mover of the Resolution, I should have expected some provision whereby it would have been possible for the state to make economic, social and political justice a reality and I should have from that point of view expected the Resolution to state in most explicit terms that in order that there may be social and economic justice in the country, that there would be nationalisation of industry and nationalisation of land, I do not understand how it could be possible for any future government which believes in doing justice socially, economically and politically, unless its economy is a socialistic economy. Therefore, personally, although I have no objection to the enunciation of these propositions, the Resolution is, to my mind, somewhat disappointing. I am however prepared to leave this subject where it is with the observations I have made."[12]

Fundamental rights are universally applicable throughout the country. They are uniformly applicable, which means they are available to all persons, irrespective of the place where they are. Uniformity also ensures that they should not be deprived of protection of fundamental rights based on social and political status or place of birth. The contents of the rights and the consequences for their violation are the same, irrespective of the place where the citizens reside. According to Dr. Ambedkar, fundamental rights under the Constitution are uniform throughout India and enforceable against all authorities exercising authority under different subjects under the Constitution.[13] It is natural to expect that all citizens have fundamental rights, otherwise the very idea of fundamental rights would be defeated. It is immaterial which part of the country the citizens lived in. They all possess the same kind and quality of fundamental rights. In Jammu & Kashmir this constitutional principle des not apply. Citizens of

India and some groups in Jammu & Kashmir are deprived of their fundamental rights in the state. The details of these two categories of persons who are deprived of fundamental rights are discussed in the following section.

Dr. Ambedkar wanted the entire governmental system to be accountable for violation of fundamental rights. Governments at all levels of constitutional structure are responsible for upholding and protecting fundamental rights. Every authority is duty-bound to respect fundamental rights. Authority is defined broadly in the Constitution to mean: "... Every authority which has got either the power to make laws or the power to have discretion invested in it."[14] It was necessary and practical to define authority broadly so that it includes all levels of governance. The Central Government, state governments (including the then provinces and erstwhile princely states), district local boards, municipalities, village Panchayats and *Taluk* boards are included. Dr. Ambedkar couched the provisions in such a form that "in fact, every authority which has been created by law and which has got certain power to make laws, to make rules, or make by-laws" would be covered.[15] He conceptualised universal application of fundamental rights against all authorities that are created by law. Fundamental rights would lose their relevance if they were not made universal and made applicable against all authorities exercising governmental power in one way or another. The making of maximum number authorities accountable shows the seriousness with which Dr. Ambedkar considered fundamental rights.

Uniform and universal application of fundamental rights in the Constitution was a watershed provision. As was discussed in Chapter 2, there was wide gap between provinces and princely states. In princely states, involvement of people in the political system was either limited or completely absent. By limiting powers of government, fundamental rights ensure that governments are accountable to people. For princely states and even for provinces this was a revolutionary thought.

For the first time, through fundamental rights all persons across the country were politically empowered. In addition to political empowerment, there was a commitment to their social and economic progress as well.

Unfortunately in Jammu & Kashmir, all these foundational contents of fundamental rights set out by Dr. Ambedkar are defeated.

Jammu & Kashmir and Fundamental Rights

Dr. Ambedkar's vision of fundamental rights has been uniformly applied and respected across India. On occasions where attempts are made by the political establishment to interfere with this vision, courts have stepped in to protect fundamental rights. The track record of Indian legal system has been impressive and acclaimed internationally. It is also followed by other jurisdictions.[16]

The attitude of sensitivity and reverence towards fundamental rights prevailing in the entire country is unfortunately not accepted in Jammu & Kashmir. The practice in the state has been to violate fundamental rights. There are two sets of people whose rights are violated in Jammu & Kashmir: residents of rest of India and some residents from within the state. The trampling of fundamental rights is not a factual occurrence; rather a happening by misusing and abusing the constitutional mechanics. This is a consequence of two groups of provisions contained in the Constitution of Jammu & Kashmir and the Constitution of India, as amended by President of India through Constitution (Application to Jammu & Kashmir) Order, 1954.

Under the Constitution of Jammu & Kashmir all rights contained in the Constitution of India accrue only to permanent residents. Section 10 states:

"Section 10: Rights of the Permanent Residents

The permanent residents of the State shall have all the rights guaranteed to them under the Constitution of India."

Thus rights under the Constitution of India are limited

only for permanent residents. Other residents of the state and residents of other parts of India who are not permanent residents are not entitled to any rights.

The deprivation of fundamental rights has been achieved through the Constitution (Application to Jammu & Kashmir) Order, 1954. Article 35 was added to the Constitution of India to exclude the operation of fundamental rights in Jammu & Kashmir, except for permanent residents.

Article 35A declares that it is created to protect laws that are made to violate fundamental rights. Article 13 of the Indian Constitution says that no laws shall be passed that violates fundamental rights. Article 35A violates this solemn promise. In the case of 35A, fundamental rights have been negated and made powerless. The act of incorporating Article 35A is a grossly unconstitutional act. It is a direct affront to the desire of Dr. Ambedkar that the government of future respects fundamental rights. In this case, it is not just that the government is acting contrary to fundamental rights with impunity, rather the government of state of Jammu & Kashmir is given an authorisation to violate fundamental rights. The President does not give by amending the Constitution but by simply issuing an order to this authorisation.

More than the manner in which Article 35A exists, what it does is appalling. Article 35A is an outright mandate to violate fundamental rights. It provides as under:

"35A. Saving of laws with respect to permanent residents and their rights—Notwithstanding anything contained in this Constitution, no existing law in force in the state of Jammu & Kashmir, and no law hereafter enacted by the Legislature of the State,—

(a) Defining the classes of persons who are, or shall be, permanent residents of the state of Jammu & Kashmir; or

(b) Conferring on such permanent residents any special rights and privileges or imposing upon other persons any restrictions as respects—

(i) Employment under the State Government;
(ii) Acquisition of immovable properly in the State;
(iii) Settlement in the State; or
(iv) Right to scholarships and such other forms of aid as the State Government may provide, shall be void on the ground that it is inconsistent with or takes away or abridges any rights conferred on the other citizens of India by any provision of this Part."

What Article 35A seeks to do is evident from the language employed in the provision. Article 35A blatantly states the objective: protections of actions by the state government that violate fundamental rights. According to Article 12 of the Constitution, if a law is contrary to fundamental rights by any authority, then that law is unconstitutional. The title of Article 35A establishes that this provision in added to the Constitution of India to 'save', that is, protect laws made specially for the interest of permanent residents of Jammu & Kashmir. (The meaning of permanent residents and associated problems is discussed below in this chapter.) The article commences with the announcement that irrespective of any other provision in the Constitution of India, any law that is existing in Jammu & Kashmir or would be enacted thereafter would be void, i.e. unconstitutional because it takes away or abridges fundamental rights.

The word 'shall' is used. Thereby a strict mandate is awarded in favour of laws passed in the state. The Article then specifies what kind of laws are protected even when they are in violation of fundamental rights. First, the freedom to decide who are permanent residents is reserved by the state. No one can object why the state has chosen to call only a certain category of persons as permanent residents and not others. The state can even arbitrarily decide the limits and no one can object. By leaving the discretion of deciding the definition of permanent resident with the state government, the state government is given the right to control the category of persons to whom fundamental rights shall be granted. There is no reference to other residents of the state.

As would be discussed in the following section, in Jammu & Kashmir this very warning of Dr. Ambedkar is sidelined. The fundamental rights have been left to the mercy of the state government. What the Central Government cannot do, can be done by the state government. A natural outcome of leaving the discretion with the state government is violation of fundamental rights.

The state government can confer further "special rights and privileges" on permanent residents. The concept of permanent resident and Section 6 of the Jammu & Kashmir State Constitution was discussed in detail in the last chapter. At the time of making of the Constitution, considering the colonial past and the hierarchical system in India created due to caste, the objective was to destroy all special rights and privileges. It is unfathomable that the Constitution of India that abhorred any claim of superiority by one citizen over another by even abolishing all titles is disregarded and under the same Constitution a category of 'special and privileged' group is created. All Indians are equal and no one can claim special rights and privileges under the constitutional framework of India. Claim of special rights and privileges by any group of persons is contrary to the promise of equality. Article 35A does not stop at granting special rights and privileges. It goes further to protect laws that the state government would make for imposing restrictions on the rights of others. The Constitution does not and cannot allow using the Constitution to actively limit and violate fundamental rights of others.

The Constitution of India recognised two situations where fundamental rights could be limited: progressive legislations and affirmative action. Progressive legislations are those laws made by Parliament to achieve equitable distribution of wealth between society. These laws were required in the early years of the new Indian republic. These laws aimed at equitable distribution of wealth. Caps were imposed on the extent of holding so that the *zamindari* system can be abolished. Likewise, the tillers of lands who were in fact cultivating land were declared owners. Many such laws were made. These laws contradict fundamental rights, but they were protected. This protection was introduced through Articles 31 A to D. These articles were added to the Constitution by the Constitution (First Amendment) Act 1951 and Constitution (Fourth Amendment) Act 1955. The amendment was made to the Constitution by the Parliament after duly following the procedure under Article 368. The President did not make these amendments. Nor were the amendments made by any other authority not permitted under the Constitution to amend.

Eventually a lot of tinkering happened with these provisions in the decade of 70s during the rule of Smt. Indira Gandhi. Constitution amendments were challenged before the courts. The courts upheld fundamental rights. The Supreme Court has repeatedly held that the action of executive in immunising a law from judicial review is not absolute. The judiciary has the power to review all laws and check if they violate fundamental rights, even if the executive declares that these laws cannot be reviewed by courts.[17] The decisions are landmark since they ensure that the executive does not make laws that take away fundamental rights.

The Supreme Court has upheld affirmative action. In affirmative action, the government can make laws for granting reservation in employment and promotions in favour of 'socially and educationally backward'. The Supreme Court has permitted special provisions only in favour of these categories and no other.[18] However, the Supreme Court has not allowed actively depriving other communities of their rights. The Constitution allows special provisions being made only for 'socially and educationally backward' communities and no other. Thus making special provisions for any other community under the Constitution is not allowed. Even where the Constitution allows taking affirmative action through special provisions, it does not allow positively discriminating and taking away rights of others. Constitution does not allow exclusion of socially and educationally advanced communities from public employment. Article 35 A commits both sins: giving privileges to a category and sanctioning active deprivation of fundamental rights of other communities.

The beauty of fundamental rights is that it also consists of the mechanism for enforcement of fundamental rights. Realising the importance of fundamental rights, the mechanism specified is by itself a fundamental right. The responsibility of enforcing the rights is reposed in the highest court in our country, that is, the Supreme Court of India.[19]

Dr. Ambedkar was aware that mere stipulation of rights without effective enforcement mechanisms would make the rights an empty formality. In the early days of the Constituent Assembly, a Resolution was moved to set out the objectives that the Constitution intended to achieve. Article 32 of the Constitution provides that any person whose fundamental rights have been violated can approach the Supreme Court for protection of these rights. Dr. Ambedkar, very beautifully articulated the importance of this provision in the Constituent Assembly. Fundamental rights very coveted by him. According to him the mere presence of rights was insufficient. Effective means for achieving rights is important; otherwise the rights would become ineffective.[20] Expressing the importance of Article 32, he said:

"Sir, there is one other observation which I would like to make. In the course of the debates that have taken place in this House, both on the Directive Principles and on the Fundamental Rights, I have listened to speeches made by many members complaining that we have not enunciated a certain right or a certain policy in our Fundamental Rights or in our Directive Principles. References have been made to the Constitution of Russia and to the constitutions of other countries where such declarations, as members have sought to introduce by means of amendments, have found a place. Sir, I think I might say without meaning any offence to anybody, who has made himself responsible for these amendments that (I prefer the British method of dealing with rights. The

British method is a peculiar method, a very real and a very sound method.) British jurisprudence insists that there can be no right unless the Constitution provides a remedy for it. It is the remedy that makes a right real. If there is no remedy, there is no right at all, and I am therefore not prepared to burden the Constitution with a number of pious declarations which may sound as glittering generalities but for which the Constitution makes no provision by way of a remedy. It is much better to be limited in the scope of our rights and to make them real by enunciating remedies than to have a lot of pious wishes embodied in the Constitution. I am very glad that this House has seen that the remedies that we have provided constitute a fundamental part of this Constitution. Sir, with these words I commend this article to the House."[21]

The operation of such an important provision is excluded in Jammu & Kashmir by Article 35A.

Article 35A is the pillar of unconstitutional activities in the state of Jammu & Kashmir, introduced through the Constitution (Applicable to Jammu & Kashmir) Order, 1954. The procedural impropriety in the manner of introduction of Presidential Order, 1954 was discussed in detail in the last chapter. The last chapter discussed the unconstitutional mechanism of amending the Constitution that was resorted to defeat the sanctity reposed on the Parliament by Dr. Ambedkar through the Presidential Order 1954. Here the discussion is on the meaning of interpretation of Article 35A and the impact that it has had on fundamental rights.

Article 35A is an enigma. If one looks up any bare act of the Indian Constitution, most of the books do not contain this provision. One finds Article 35 'small' a, but one cannot find 'capital' A. This is so because Article 35 'capital' A does not exist in the Indian Constitution as applied to India. It exists in the Indian Constitution as applied to Jammu & Kashmir. It is unfathomable how one version of Indian Constitution applies to Jammu & Kashmir and another to the rest of India. The manner in which the President of India has applied the Constitution of India to Jammu & Kashmir in piecemeal is arbitrary. Moreover, it is a doubt on the wisdom of the Constituent Assembly of India and Dr. Ambedkar. Dr. Ambedkar and his colleagues in the Constituent Assembly had finalised the Constitution with great alacrity and sagacity. If the provisions of the Indian Constitution, especially on fundamental rights are good for the entire country, then why not for Jammu & Kashmir? The President of India or the state of Jammu & Kashmir, with whose consent the Constitution has been tinkered with, have cared to give reasons as to why certain provisions of the Constitution are unacceptable and inappropriate for the state of Jammu & Kashmir.

The Constitution (Application to Jammu & Kashmir) Order, 1954 was issued Article 370 (1). Article 370 was inserted into the Constitution as a temporary feature. In that capacity measures could not be taken to defeat the fundamental rights. Article 370 is only a mechanism for extending the provisions of the Indian Constitution and laws passed by the Parliament to Jammu & Kashmir. There is no foundation under Article 370 to defeat fundamental rights. Despite this position, Article 370 has been misused and abused to defeat fundamental rights of residents of Jammu & Kashmir and residents of other parts of India. In addition to circumventing the Parliament to amend the Constitution, Constitution (Application to Jammu & Kashmir) Order, 1954 goes a step further and violates fundamental rights. The central provision that blatantly violates fundamental rights without any qualm is Article 35A, added through the Constitution (Application to Jammu & Kashmir) Order, 1954.

The kinds of special provisions that have been made under Article 35A are far reaching. In addition to the absolute unchallenged discretion to decide who shall be permanent resident, the state of Jammu & Kashmir can make special provisions for i) employment in the state government, ii) acquisition of immovable property, iii) settlement in the state and iv) scholarships and other aids provided by the state government.

i) ***Employment***

Employment in departments of the state government is limited exclusively for the permanent residents. Other residents of Jammu & Kashmir that do not have the permanent resident certificate are not allowed to enter employment in the state government. The irony is that a person from any other part of India can join the Central Civil Service such as Indian Administrative Service or Indian Police Service, and be employed in Jammu & Kashmir in that capacity. But a person from the rest of India cannot join the state administrative service or any other position in the employment of the state government. In other words, a citizen of India without permanent resident certificate can become a District Collector in Jammu & Kashmir but cannot become a clerk in that very department.

ii) ***Acquisition of immovable property:***

Except for permanent residents, no other person can own property in Jammu & Kashmir. Thus the categories of persons described above that have lived in the state for decades are not allowed to own property. The regime of permanent resident is a form of licence/ police raj.

Special rights to own property, granted exclusively in favour of permanent residents, is contrary to the Indian Constitution. When the Constitution was drafted, right to property was a fundamental right. Uniformity of fundamental rights ensured that any person residing in any part of India could hold property in Jammu & Kashmir. But thorough Article 35 A, this right was defeated. The right to property was removed from fundamental rights through the Constitution (Forty-Fourth Amendment) Act, 1978. This Constitutional Amendment was not made applicable to Jammu & Kashmir. Therefore, right to property continues to exist in Jammu & Kashmir. Right to property continues to exist as a legal right under Indian Constitution Article 300A. In Jammu & Kashmir the right is not available either as a fundamental right or a constitutional right to anyone except permanent residents.

The restriction on the rights of non-permanent residents to hold property has impacted business and industry. No person without the privileged permanent resident status can buy property and set up an industry in Jammu & Kashmir. The discretion of making an exception to the rule for allowing industry is with the state government. This discretion has allowed the despicable licence/ police raj prevailing in India prior to 1992 to continue in Jammu & Kashmir.

iii) ***Settlement in the State***

The right to settle in the state is limited exclusively for permanent residents. In order to settle, one has to be entitled to purchase property. The bar on purchasing property ensures that non-permanent residents cannot settle in the state. Since 'others' cannot settle in the state, they cannot practice any profession or seek permanent employment in the state. For practicing law in Jammu & Kashmir, registration is required. Registration would not take place if the applicant is not a permanent resident.

iv) ***Scholarship and other governmental aids:***

Scholarships are necessary to facilitate education for bright students who cannot otherwise afford education due to their financial situation. In case of such students, it ought to be immaterial whether they or their parents have a permanent resident certificate. All that matters is that they have stayed in the state and are in need of financial support. Students belonging to marginalised communities are not eligible for consideration of scholarships for the simple reason that they do not have permanent resident status. For example the Prime Minister has instituted a scholarship for students from Jammu & Kashmir to study in other parts of India. The scholarship can be availed only if the applicant is a permanent resident.

This rule is applied to all governmental aids. The net of this limitation has been extended not only to the state government schemes but even to Central Government schemes. Most of the Central Government schemes have a share of the state government and are implemented by the state government. Non-permanent residents are deprived benefits of all these schemes.

v) ***Extension to other rights***

Although Article 35A allows infringement of fundamental rights to four categories, in fact there are many other rights in relation to which rights of non-permanent resident certificate-holders are subject to discrimination in many other fields.

The permanent resident is required to conduct most of the activities for earning livelihood. In order to obtain contracts of public works in the state of Jammu & Kashmir the Jammu & Kashmir Registration of Contractors Act, 1956 is in operation. Under Section 3 of the Act, registration of a contractor is made mandatory. The registration rules require that the application shall have a permanent resident certificate. In order to become a dealer, registration is required under Section 27 of the Jammu & Kashmir State Value Added Tax, 2005. The prescribed format for registration, as per the rules, requires that the applicant shall be a permanent resident. To work as a tourist operator or run a hotel, registration is required under Sections 3 and 9 respectively of the Jammu & Kashmir Registration of Tourist Trade Act, 1989. Rules have been framed under these Sections which also require permanent resident certificate. Even a self-reliant co-operative society cannot be formed because even to register as a co-operative society, as per Section 16 (a) (ii) of the Jammu & Kashmir Self-Reliant Co-operatives Act, 1999 one has to be a permanent resident. In order to constitute a co-operative society, Section 17 of the Jammu & Kashmir Co-operative Societies Act, 1989 requires that in order to become a member, the person shall be a permanent resident.

It is shocking to note that even to avail benefits as a disabled person being a permanent resident is mandatory. The government of Jammu & Kashmir has powers to make schemes under Section 32 of the Jammu & Kashmir Persons with Disabilities (Equal Opportunities, Protection of Rights and Full Participation) Act, 1998. Schemes made thereunder for mentally and physically disabled are limited only for permanent residents.

Political participation is a very important right. The communities that do not have fundamental rights in Jammu & Kashmir are deprived of political participation. An important right necessary for political participation is the right of voting. The Jammu & Kashmir Representation of People's Act limits the right of voting for permanent residents. Section12 (1) (b) of the Jammu & Kashmir Representation of People's Act, 1957 disqualifies a person from registration in electoral roll if the person is not a permanent resident. Since non-permanent residents are not on electoral roll, they are not allowed to contest elections for the Legislative Assembly and Legislative Council by virtue of Sections 22 and 23 respectively. Travesty is that different categories of persons that stay in Jammu & Kashmir and do not have permanent resident certificate can vote in parliamentary elections but they cannot vote in state or Panchayat elections. The situation is unfathomable; one resides in a place and has been residing for decades, but one does not belong to such a place. The feeling of alienation and infringement of rights perpetrated under Article 35A is troublesome.

The Directive Principles of State Policy are an advise to the future governments about the laws that could be made. The Constitution of Jammu & Kashmir contains these provisions. These provisions are limited for the benefit of permanent residents. Additionally, the Directive Principles of State Policy in the Jammu & Kashmir State Constitution make provisions only for permanent residents.

The Directive Principles of State Policy in the Jammu & Kashmir Constitution are also unreasonably bent in favour of permanent residents and exclude welfare measures for others.

"Section 19: Right to work and to public assistance in certain cases:- The State shall, within the limits of its economic capacity and development, make effective provision for securing –

(a) that all permanent residents, men and women

equally, have the right to work, that is, the right to receive guaranteed work with payment for labour in accordance with its quantity and quality, subject to a basic minimum and maximum wage established by law;

(b) that the health and strength of workers, men and women and the tender-age of children are not abused and that permanent residents are not forced by economic necessity to enter avocations unsuited to their sex, age or strength;

(c) that all workers, agricultural, industrial or otherwise, have reasonable, just and humane conditions of work with full enjoyment of leisure and social and cultural opportunities;

(d) that all permanent residents have adequate maintenance in old age as well as in the event of sickness, disablement, unemployment and other cases of undeserved want by providing social insurance, medical aid, hospitals, sanatoria and health resorts at State expense.

"Section 20: Rights of free and compulsory education in certain cases:- The State shall endeavour–

(a) to secure to every permanent resident the right to free education up to the university standard;

(b) to provide, within a period of ten years from the commencement of this Constitution, compulsory education for all children until they complete the age of fourteen years; and

(c) to ensure to all workers and employees adequate facilities for adult education and part-time technical, professional and vocational courses."

Broadly there are two categories of Indian citizens who are deprived of fundamental rights and special discriminatory rights could be given to permanent residents by excluding these two categories. The first category is of citizens of India residing in other parts of India. As was discussed above, fundamental rights are universal. They are available throughout India. But in Jammu & Kashmir, if a citizen of India is not a permanent resident of the state, then fundamental rights are unavailable. Therefore, an Indian citizen who is not a permanent resident cannot settle, do a business or profession, gain technical education, etc. The second category is of residents of the state of Jammu & Kashmir who are not permanent residents. Some of them have been residing in Jammu & Kashmir from much prior to integration of Jammu & Kashmir, i.e. during the rule of Dogra kings. During this time, they were state subjects but after coming into force of the Constitution of Jammu & Kashmir, they have not been given permanent resident status. Some came after 1947 in the state, but they too have been residing in the state for more than three or four generations. Yet they are not given permanent resident certificate and are therefore excluded from protection of fundamental rights. They include women, persons belonging to Valmiki community (sweepers or *safai karmacharis,* mostly Dalit), Gorkhas residing in the state of Jammu & Kashmir and West Pakistan refugees. This category also includes women. The situation of women is slightly different. They have fundamental rights which are destroyed in certain situations. Details of deprivation of rights of all these groups of persons are discussed hereunder.

a) ***Women***

The social structure of India degraded so much with time that women have been subjected to mistreatment. It was necessary to correct this social evil through constitutional mechanisms. Therefore a provision for equal rights for women became necessary. Article 14 generally recognises that no discrimination can be made between any two individuals. Articles 15 and 16 provide specific protection. They protect rights of women more precisely. They dictate that there shall be no discrimination based on sex.

Dr. Ambedkar may not have expressed any direct views on equality of men and women, but his general comments on fundamental rights adequately express his commitment towards gender equality. The constitutional guarantee of gender equality has been successfully invoked in the entire country. The situation in Jammu & Kashmir is not the same. The state government has repeatedly and with success deprived women from equal rights as compared to men in the state. The state government issued a clarification stating that the permanent certificate of a woman would expire once she marries a non-permanent resident. This clarification was challenged before the Jammu & Kashmir High Court. The court struck down the interpretation and held that a woman would not lose her permanent resident status by marrying a non-permanent resident.[22] The political establishment was unhappy with this decision. A Bill was introduced in the Legislative Council to undo the decision – called 'The Jammu & Kashmir Permanent Resident (Disqualification) Bill 2004'.[23] The Bill disqualifies women from permanent resident status once they marry a non-permanent resident. The Preamble of the Bill says that it is "[a] Bill to provide for disqualification from being a permanent resident of the state on marriage of a female permanent resident with a non-permanent resident." The Legislative Assembly unanimously passed the Bill without debate within minutes on 5 March 2004.[24] However, the Bill could not be passed in the Legislative Council because the Chairman of the Legislative Council adjourned the House *sine die*.[25] If the Bill resurfaces or any similar Bill is passed, then women marrying men outside the state of Jammu & Kashmir will lose their permanent resident certificate.

This is not the only form of discrimination that women face. The children born out of a wedding between a permanent resident wife and non-permanent resident husband are not entitled for permanent resident certificate. If the man is a permanent resident and he marries a non-permanent resident, she and her children get all rights of permanent resident. The Supreme Court has consistently upheld the rights of children, whether born out of a legal wedlock or not.[26] But in the case of Jammu & Kashmir, children born to a permanent resident mother and non permanent resident father do not get any rights and privileges of a permanent resident. Needless to say, the non-permanent resident husband does not get permanent resident status even if he stays in the state.

b) ***Valmiki Community & Gorkhas***

The traumatising story is of persons residing in the state of Jammu & Kashmir that belong to the Valmiki community and are forced to do the job of sweepers in the state of Jammu & Kashmir. Most of them are Dalits. In 1957, in Jammu & Kashmir there was a strike of sweepers/cleaners in government employment. The government dismissed them from service and in their place decided to bring sweepers/ cleaners from Punjab. They were promised that they would be given permanent resident certificate. There were over 250 families that relocated based on that promise.[27] According to Section 35 B of the Jammu & Kashmir Civil Service Regulations, "Every new entrant into government service, the authority empowered to make the appointment should certify that the person appointed is a hereditary state subject." According to Exemption 1, sweepers are exempted from producing the certificate of state subject. For any of the persons working as sweepers or their family members, the only job that is open is of a sweeper. They cannot seek any other job in the state government despite the fact that they have been residing in the State for more than 60 years. They cannot obtain any other employment with the state government. They are not entitled for promotions.[28] Since they are allowed employment only as a sweepers without being a hereditary state subject, despite the fact their colleagues who are hereditary state subjects are promoted to higher posts, while persons from Valmiki community are not. The exception is made only as long as they are working as sweepers. They have to remain at the same position all their life and their juniors get promoted. The situation of their children is precarious. They are not entitled to any of the privileges of permanent residents except for being *safai karmachari* (cleaner/ sweeper). They may get best of the education and degrees but they cannot aspire to be anything more than a sweeper in the state. This is a modern form of slavery being practiced in one state of India. These grave violations of fundamental rights are taking place despite a progressive Constitution. Thus excluding their promotion, this is a shocking form of slavery practiced in the state of Jammu & Kashmir.

Similar is the plight of persons from Gorkha community that reside in the state. Section 35 B of the Jammu & Kashmir Service Regulations, Exception 1 contains another exception of retired Gorkhas that are enlisted to work as *chowkidars.* They too are placed in a similar situation as *safai karmacharis* (sweepers) because they to are allowed to be employed without the state subject certificate. People from the Gorkha community have been staying in the state from much before 1947. Somewhere around mid-of ninenteenth century (around 1848), they came to Jammu & Kashmir from Nepal. They were inducted into the army of Maharaja Gulab Singh and fought battles in the Army of Maharaja Ranbir Singh, Maharaja Pratap Singh and Maharaja Hari Singh. They played a major role in the present territorial structure of Jammu & Kashmir.

While the concept of state subject existed during the time of Dogra rulers, they had all the rights under the rule of Maharaja. In 1957 when permanent resident was defined to exclude some categories of state subjects, they too were excluded. All their rights were suddenly deprived without any intimation to them. Some of them continue to own properties that they had acquired prior to 1957, yet they do not have any powers of permanent resident.[29]

For the past 60 years, Valmikis and Gorkhas are being subjected to slavery and servitude, depriving them and their coming generations of possibility of progress.

c) ***West Pak Refugees***

The Partition of India in 1947 created an immense human tragedy. People from different parts of present Pakistan came to India as refugees. There are a group of persons that came from the Sialkot district of Pakistan, which is also known as Western Pakistan. From all the people that came, some of them were promised to stay back in Jammu & Kashmir by the then Prime Minister of Jammu & Kashmir Sheikh Abdullah. He requested them to stay back in the state and not go further into India. They were asked to stay in the areas adjoining the boundary between India and Pakistan which had become vacant due to exodus of people from those areas during Partition. When they came they were 5764 families. With time their number has increased and they are presently 30,000 families and around 2 lakh people. They have lived in the state since 1947 but are not given permanent resident status and thereby deprived of all rights and privileges that permanent residents are entitled to. Their fourth generation is suffering the pain. Some of them approached the Supreme Court. The court recognised their plight and directed the state and the Central Government to look into their situation and take appropriate steps. The Supreme Court said:

> "In the circumstances, in view of the peculiar constitutional position obtaining in the state of Jammu & Kashmir, we do not see what possible relief we can give to the Petitioner and those situated like him. All that we can say is that the position of the Petitioner and those like him is anomalous and it is up to the legislature of the state of Jammu & Kashmir to take action to amend legislations, such as the Jammu & Kashmir Representation of the People's Act, the Land Acquisition Act, the Village Panchayat Act, etc. so as to make persons like the Petitioner who have migrated from West Pakistan in 1947 and who have settled down in the state of Jammu & Kashmir since then, eligible to be included in the electoral roll, to acquire land, to be elected to the Panchayat, etc. etc. This can be done by suitably amending the legislations without having to amend the Jammu & Kashmir Constitution. In regard to providing employment opportunities under the State Government, it can be done by the government by amending the Jammu & Kashmir Civil Services,

> Classification, Control and Appeal Riles. In regard to the admission to higher technical educational institutions also, the government may make these persons eligible by issuing appropriate executive directions without even having to introduce any legislation. The Petitioners have a justifiable grievance. We are told that they constitute nearly seven to eight per cent of the population of the state of Jammu & Kashmir. Surely they are entitled to expect to be protected by the state of Jammu & Kashmir. In the peculiar context of the state of Jammu & Kashmir, the Union of India also owes an obligation to make some provision for the advancement of the cultural, economic and educational rights of these persons. We do hope that the claims of persons like the Petitioner and others to greater rights of citizenship will receive due consideration from the Union of India and the state of Jammu & Kashmir. We are, however, unable to give any relief to the Petitioners."[30]

However till today nothing has been done in this regard. A Parliamentary Committee Report of Rajya Sabha has also gone into the issue and sympathised with their plight. The Report said:

The Committee expresses its serious concern that the West Pakistani refugees, who are very much citizens of India and eligible for voting in parliamentary elections, do not possess right to vote in the State Legislative Assembly elections on the pretext that they are not permanent residents of the state in terms of the J&K Constitution. The committee feels that though they are living there for more than 60 years, they are not leading the life of free citizens despite having voting rights for Parliament. This right has not earned them any special benefits.

The Committee strongly recommends that the Central Government must impress upon the state government to consider, as a one-time measure, the demand of West Pakistani refugees to grant them the status of permanent residents of the state sympathetically so that they can live as state subject in a dignified way, with all legal rights including right to vote in State Legislative Assembly."

Despite these repeated observations, their situation has not improved.

Stories of these communities are in public; therefore they are identified. It is possible that there are other categories of persons, whose fundamental rights visualised by Dr. Ambedkar and guaranteed under the Constitution are violated.

When Dr. Ambedkar powerfully spoke about the importance of fundamental rights, it was the protection of such vulnerable groups. The constitutional machinery has failed to uphold the obligation he imposed on the state government to follow. The effect of Article 35 A is that there are two categories of Indian citizens created in Jammu & Kashmir: one that holds permanent resident certificate and another that does not. The wedge created between the two categories, although both are Indian citizens – violates the basic principles of equality.

It leaves no doubt that the situation in Jammu & Kashmir is contrary to constitutional values that Dr. Ambedkar thought were the best for a secure future of this country. These values, especially on fundamental rights, have proved to be successful in the entire country. Thus one cannot even doubt the credibility and effectiveness of these values but in Jammu & Kashmir these values are disregarded and disrespected. Through the misuse of Article 370, Article 35A is used to destroy the constitutional guarantee of fundamental rights which was very dear to Dr. Ambedkar.

The question is not who bears the blame and responsibility for the situation in Jammu & Kashmir, the fact of the day is that it has become a ground for blatant violation of fundamental rights with impunity and defeating Dr. Ambedkar's vision.[31]

References

1. Granville Austin, *The Indian Constitution: Cornerstone of a Nation*. OUP, (1999), p. 63
2. Ibid, pp. 76-86
3. Chandrima Das vs. Railway Welfare Board, (2000) 2 SCC 465

4. This movement began with the case Maneka Gandhi vs. Union of India (1978) 1 SCC 248. Many cases thereafter have expanded the scope of fundamental rights thereafter. See generally Udai Raj Rai, '*Fundamental Rights and Their Enforcement*', PHI Learning Pvt Ltd (2011)
5. See P D Mathew, *Fundamental Rights in Action*, Indian Social Institute (1996): Udai Raj Rai, *Fundamental Rights and Their Enforcement* (PHI Learning Pvt. Ltd., 2011); M P Jain, *Indian Constitutional Law* (6th edn, revised by Samaraditya Pal and Ruma Pal; Vol.2 Lexis Nexis Butterworths Wadhwa (2010), pp. 1175-1952
6. People's Union for Civil Liberties vs. Union of India (2005) 2 SCC 436
7. Minerva Mills Ltd. vs. Union of India, (1980) 2 SCC 591; Kesavananda Bharati vs. State of Kerala (1973) 4 SCC 225
8. M. Nagaraj vs. Union of India, (2006), 8 SCC 212
9. Constituent Assembly Debates Official Report (*CAD*), Reprint by Lok Sabha Secretariat, New Delhi (2009), Book 1, p. 100
10. Ibid, p. 275
11. *CAD*, Book 2, p. 610
12. Above note 9, p. 100
13. Above note 11, p. 957
14. Ibid, p. 610
15. Ibid
16. For an excellent account of working of the Indian Constitution *see* Granville Austin, *Working in a Democratic Constitution: A History of the Indian Experience*, OUP India (2003)
17. Waman Rao vs. Union of India, (1981) 2 SCC 362; I. R. Coelho vs. State of Kerala, (2007) 2 SCC 1
18. M.R. Balaji vs. State of Mysore, (1963) Supplementary (1) SCR 439; Indira Sawhney vs. Union of India, 1992 Supplementary (3) SCC 217; State of Uttar Pradesh vs. Pradeep Tandon, (1975) 1 SCC 267; Ashok Kumar Thakur vs. Union of India, (2008) 6 SCC 1
19. Article 32, Constitution of India
20. Above note 9, p. 100
21. Above note 10, pp. 953-4
22. Dr. Susheela Sawhney vs. State of Jammu & Kashmir (LPA 29/279), Dr. Rubina Nasarullah vs. State of J&K (OWP No. 152/1985), Shabnam Taj vs. State of Jammu & Kashmir (OWP 52/97)

23. Article 370: *Deceit and Fraudulent Communication,* Sant Kumar Sharma, Makhanlal Chaturvedi National University of Journalism & Communication, Bhopal (2016), p. 72
24. For a detailed factual account of what happened in the two Legislative Assembly and Council *see* Hari Om, '*Daughters of J & K: India's most Unwanted,* 12 March 2010, available at: http://www.vijayvaani.com/ArticleDisplay.aspx?aid=1132
25. The action of the Chairman led to a political storm and was expelled from his own party for not having facilitated the passing of the Bill. *See* TNS and UNI,; NC Expels Dar, blames Mufti for 'sabotaging' Bill', Srinagar, March 12, 2004, available at: http://www.tribuneindia.com/2004/20040313/j&k.htm#2; last visited: 28 December 2016
26. Revanasiddappa vs. Mallikarjun 2011 (86) ALR 450
27. Dinesh Manhotra, 'Independence means nothing for Valmiki community of Jammu', *Tribune News Service,* Jammu, 12 August 2016, available at: http://www.tribuneindia.com/news/jammu-kashmir/independence-means-nothing-for-valmiki-community-of-jammu/279767.html; last visited: 28 December 2016
28. Sonali Chitalkar, 'How Article 35-A has been creating havoc in Jammu & Kashmir', 2 December 2016, available at: http://www.jammukashmirnow.com/Encyc/2016/12/2/-Article-35-A; last visited: 28 December 2016
29. Major K. Brahma singh (Retd), *History of Jammu & Kashmir Rifles 1820-1956,* Lancer International (1990), p. 21
30. Bachan Lal Kalgotra vs. State of J & K in (1987) 2 SCC 223, para 5
31. Rajya Sabha, department related to Parliamentary Standing Committee on Home Affairs, 183rd Reported "problems being faced by refugees and displaced persons in J & K (22nd December, 2014)

❒

8

Conclusion

The discussion in the preceding pages has shown that Dr. Ambedkar had a very clear and specific idea of India. This idea was shared by all the members of the Constituent Assembly, which included representatives of all the former princely states, including those from the state of Jammu & Kashmir. The representatives of Jammu & Kashmir participated and supported the making of that vision. However, in practical terms, the situation in the state of Jammu & Kashmir is contrary to the legal and constitutional vision of Dr. Ambedkar.

It is not only pertinent but indispensable to understand Dr. Ambedkar's vision for modern India, especially in the context of the manner in which things have unfolded in the state of Jammu & Kashmir. Dr. Ambedkar made vital contributions to the making of the Indian Constitution and the structures that followed. Therefore, while analysing the problems in the state of Jammu & Kashmir it becomes important to recollect his vision for India. He had a clear vision about the future of princely states in modern India. He was opposed to the idea of lapsing of paramountcy and insisted that since the Dominion of India is the succeeding State to the British Crown, the paramountcy should be transferred to India. This would have made the need of entering into Instruments of Accession redundant. He was optimistic that the princely states would join India and participate wholeheartedly in the Constitution-making process; which they did, including the state of

Jammu & Kashmir. The princely states had lagged behind democratically. He wished to ensure that true democracy is practiced and realised in these former princely states with people's participation. Dr. Ambedkar ensured that the distinction between princely states and the British provinces comes to an end in the new constitutional framework. The Constitution was structured accordingly. Although the former princely states were allowed to draft their own internal Constitution, he insisted that there should be a common Constitution-making process and should not insist on drafting a separate Constitution in the states. However, all his advices were disregarded in the state of Jammu & Kashmir. Moreover, the constitutional values that he considered to be fundamental for the Indian Constitution and for the future of Indian people have been defeated in the state.

Dr. Ambedkar was aware of the differences in the country. To keep the country together, a strong Centre was necessary. The powers of administration and governance are shared between the Centre and the states. Yet, Dr. Ambedkar created structures with strong bias towards the Centre and did not use the word federation anywhere. Thus, India is a federal structure with strong unitary bias. This was achieved by granting residual legislative powers to the Union Government. There is unified judiciary and All India Civil Service ensures that the senior officials in the states are in service with the Central Government. Also, fundamental laws, including civil and criminal laws, are uniform throughout India. The bond between the Centre and the states is much stronger in the Indian Constitution, as compared to the American Constitution. Therefore, the dual polity that exists in federal countries does not exist in India. The duality of laws, licences for professional activities, etc. which would normally exist in federal countries, are done away with in the Indian system. All these creations of Dr. Ambedkar are undone in Jammu & Kashmir. There is a separate civil and criminal code. Many provisions in these codes are far from progressive. There is duality exercised in relation to certain laws and the state claims to have residual legislative power.

Most of the powers exercised by the government of Jammu & Kashmir are claimed to be protected under Article 370. Dr Ambedkar was opposed to creation of such a provision specially for one state. He was deliberately kept out of the drafting process of Article 370 and its presentation and debate in the Constituent Assembly. In case of all provisions, Dr. Ambedkar used to introduce the provisions and then defend them. This did not happen in the case of Article 370. He did not even participate in the debate. One of the reasons for his resignation from the Union Cabinet was the manner in which Jammu & Kashmir was being handled.

Sovereignty rests with the people of India and not with any institution or any former princely state for that matter. Dr. Ambedkar said so very clearly. It is a shocking matter that claims are being made by scholars and the High Court of Jammu & Kashmir that sovereignty is shared between the Government of India and the government of the state of Jammu & Kashmir – or some sort of sovereignty has been retained by the state even after its full and final integration with India. Now the Supreme Court has upturned the decision of the High Court, whereby sovereignty was claimed to remain the state of Jammu & Kashmir.

Article 370 has been used as an instrument for defeating Dr. Ambedkar's vision. The constitutional and legal structures envisaged by Dr. Ambedkar for protecting the interest of the people, especially of deprived section and to keep the country together have been targeted and destroyed by misuse of Article 370.

Dr. Ambedkar introduced separation of powers as a founding principle of the India Constitution, whereby the powers of the three organs i.e. the Parliament, government and the judiciary are kept independent. One organ cannot usurp the powers of another. In the case of Jammu & Kashmir, this balance has been defeated. The President enjoys disproportionate powers in relation to Jammu & Kashmir. Laws made by the Parliament and the amendments made to the Constitution by the Parliament are automatically applicable to the entire country; but not in Jammu & Kashmir. In Jammu & Kashmir the President has a further power to decide whether to make Central laws and amendment to the Constitution applicable to Jammu & Kashmir or not. The President not only enjoys the power to decide which laws and constitutional amendments to apply, but can also apply them selectively and decide not to apply some of them at all.

The President's power has been used abusively and the Constitution (Application to Jammu & Kashmir) Order, 1954 is a manifest example. The Order of 1954 has disrupted many valued principles under the Indian Constitution that were dear to Dr. Ambedkar's heart. First and foremost, the Order of 1954 disturbed the distribution of legislative power between the Centre and the state legislature. The residual power that remains with the Parliament was transferred to the state legislature by the Order of 1954. If Article 370 had originally conceived retention of residual legislative powers by the state legislature, then Article 370 would have specifically said so. The Parliament could exercise residual powers till 1954, but could not exercise them after coming into force of the Order of 1954 which is irreconcilable. There are no legal justifications given for this change. The purported basis is the agreement between Pandit Nehru and Sheikh Abdullah. Dr. Ambedkar and the Constituent Assembly were clear that the Constitution was a neutral document. It could not be altered through a political agreement between two political leaders. If at all, any change to the Constitution had to be made, then it had to go through the Parliament. Changes to the Constitution cannot be made through backdoor to grant special rights in favour of one state.

The disturbing action undertaken under the Order of 1954 includes granting of special rights to residents of Jammu & Kashmir. Dr. Ambedkar was clear that there would be only single citizenship and at the most, some restrictions in the form of domicile could be issued. There could be no special treatment whatsoever for residents of a state. In Jammu & Kashmir, the residents are issued permanent resident certificate, under Section 6 of the Jammu & Kashmir Constitution. Many rights in the state are reserved exclusively for the permanent residents. Only permanent residents can exercise important rights, such as the right to vote. Thus other residents of the state can vote in parliamentary elections but cannot vote in the state or local elections. Also, the manner for granting permanent resident status is arbitrarily fixed in a manner that no other person would be entitled to claim it. It is issued only to those persons who have settled in the state prior to 14 May 1944. The discretion to grant such status has been retained by the state government.

Dr. Ambedkar was always concerned about the well-being of the marginalised and downtrodden communities. One of the reasons why he agreed to participate in the Constitution-making process at the offer of Pandit Nehru was that he was confident that he could translate those concerns into action. He had coined the word Scheduled Tribes and granted them special rights under the Constitution. These provisions have been excluded from operation in Jammu & Kashmir. Persons belonging to Scheduled Tribes residing in Jammu & Kashmir do not get the benefit reservation and other benefits that persons of those communities get in other parts of the country.

Dr. Ambedkar was very particular about fundamental rights. He considered them to be an important instrument of social transformation. He participated actively in the debates that took place on fundamental rights and rendered scholarly, practical but heart-touching speeches. The jurisprudence of the Supreme Court, especially post the judgment of Keshavananda Bharti, has taken due account of the views of Dr. Ambedkar on fundamental rights. The Order of 1954 has introduced Article 35 A in the Constitution of India as applied to Jammu & Kashmir. This is an amendment to the Constitution, which has been done by the President of India. This amendment was made to the Constitution without informing the Parliament or by following the procedure for constitutional amendments. Article 35 A excludes the operation of fundamental rights in the state of Jammu & Kashmir. It allows the state of Jammu & Kashmir to make special laws in favour of permanent residents that violates rights of other citizens. It also protects laws that violate fundamental rights and allows them to continue. Article 35 A allows the state to make special rights in favour of the permanent residents in relation to employment, education, scholarships and property. In practice, the special rights have been extended to most of the professional and business communities and other activities which have resulted in economic and social exclusion of those who reside in the state but do not have a permanent resident certificate, such as licence for government contracts, establishing shops, claiming benefits under Disabilities Act, etc. The impediments suffered by those residing in the state and who do not have a permanent resident certificate are suffered by citizens of India residing in other parts of India.

The shocking situation is of women, persons from Valmiki community (sweepers/ cleaners/ *safai karmacharis*), Gorkhas and West Pakistan Refugees. Dr. Ambedkar always stood for the struggle of these groups. They are deprived of fundamental rights in the state even after so many years of Independence. A lot of these communities are subjected to slavery, something that Dr. Ambedkar abhorred. All of it is happening under the garb of Article 370 to defeat Dr. Ambedkar's vision of India.

The discourse on Jammu & Kashmir today is muddled. If is difficult to find out what the contributors to debate really want, except for making some suggestions and controversial statements all the time. Let us assume they expect two things: complete cessation from India or autonomy or special status to the state. None of the suggestions fit in with the vision of Dr. Ambedkar, was time and again telling in the Constituent Assembly that the country had to be kept together. He was aware of the differences, and thus knew that we have to introduce robustly centralised uniform structures. The arguments of separate and special status suddenly emerged once terrorist activities started in Jammu & Kashmir in the late 80s. With the quelling of terrorism, seepage into intellectual area is ongoing with arguments supporting separatist tendencies. It is timely to consider the situation of the state in light of the vision of a great national leader, an eminent jurist and a visionary who pioneered the direction the country should take. The entire country has happily embarked upon the journey that he pointed to the country to undertake. It is only in Jammu & Kashmir where his vision is disregarded.

Solutions to all of the problems persistent in the state of Jammu & Kashmir rest on realising Dr. Ambedkar's vision. If the lawmakers and the Indian society steadfastly stays honest to the vision of India and constitutional structure of India, all associated problems with Jammu & Kashmir would automatically get resolved.

❏❏❏

Postscript

By the time this book went to press, the Presidential Order to revoke Article 370 was made. The removal of Article 370 and 35 A are an important step in achieving the vision of India as contemplated by Dr. Ambedkar.

The removal of Article 370 brings the two new Union Territories of Jammu and Kashmir and Ladakh at the same level of integration as every other State within India. As the Republic of India came into being after coming into force of the Indian Constitution, the distinction between formerly Princely States and Provinces came to an end. All the constituents achieved the same status within the Indian polity under the rubric of the constitution, as drafted and conceptualized by Dr. Ambedkar. The distinct treatment given to the State of Jammu and Kashmir was on the historic origin of the State as a Princely State. Dr. Ambedkar was opposed to the distinction between Princely States and Provinces in the independent India. Such historical antecedents had to go away in the new republic as he saw it. The distinction based on former Princely States and Provinces was unfortunate for the Princely States since they were left behind in comparison to the Provinces on democratic process and general development and progress of the people. This created an artificial distinction between people. Dr. Ambedkar was insistent that this distinction shall end soon. That vision of Dr. Ambedkar that could not be realized immediately at the time of coming into force of the

Indian Constitution has been realized now. This vision of his was shared by the members of the Drafting Committee as well as a very large majority of the Constituent Assembly. Although belatedly, the removal of this inappropriate and artificial distinction is the first step in the direction of achieving of Dr. Ambedkar's vision.

Dr. Ambedkar wished that the Centre remains strong to ensure that the integrity and unity of India is not compromised in any manner. Article 370 had reduced the extent of powers exercisable by the Centre in relation to other States. This created a situation where the nature of Centre State relations as existed in all other States was different from that in relation to Jammu and Kashmir. A situation that was a direct affront to the federal structure as created by Dr. Ambedkar and endorsed by the Drafting Committee. Removal of Article 370 will ensure that the relation of the Centre with the constituents remains the same across India. There will be uniformity of federal relations, as was Dr. Ambedkar's vision. The presence of different laws in the former State of Jammu and Kashmir that were archaic in many respects will not survive any more. All the legislations with their progressive vision will continue to apply with full force in the region.

There would be no distinction in the extent and quality of fundamental rights between persons within the former State of Jammu and Kashmir and outside the State of Jammu and Kashmir. With the demise of Article 35 A, the artificial distinction and the rights for the so-called State citizens would not exist anymore. The special provisions made for vulnerable groups, particularly Scheduled Casts and Scheduled Tribes in the Indian Constitution and legislative provisions by the Parliament were not applied in Jammu and Kashmir due to Article 370, now they will extend with full force to the region and will be important in ensuring that the historically deprived communities are allowed to grow to their fullest potential with the help of appropriate support wherever necessary.

The greatest step towards achieving Dr. Ambedkar's vision uniformly in India is in the form of application of universal application of fundamental rights in the entire country including the former State of Jammu and Kashmir. All individuals residing in the State would have equal fundamental rights and no one categories of persons would have superior rights as compared to others. Most importantly the gender based discrimination that deprived women of equal rights would not have any application any more. It is disturbing that it took more than seventy years to introduce gender equality in the former State of Jammu and Kashmir but it is better late than never!

The removal of Article 370 and the consequential discriminatory and unconstitutional provisions including Article 35 A will contribute towards achieving Dr. Ambedkar's vision of India which would be a strong country with a strong Union that could bring equality justice and progress for all Indians irrespective of their place of birth, origin and gender.

❑❑❑